Guid...

KW-334-510

VOL 26 / PART 3
September–December 2010

Commissioned by **Jeremy Duff**; *edited by* **Lisa Cherrett**

Suggestions for using *Guidelines*

Set aside a regular time and place, if possible, when you can read and pray undisturbed. Before you begin, take time to be still and, if you find it helpful, use the BRF prayer.

In *Guidelines*, the introductory section provides context for the passages or themes to be studied, while the units of comment can be used daily, weekly, or whatever best fits your timetable. You will need a Bible (more than one if you want to compare different translations) as Bible passages are not included. At the end of each week is a 'Guidelines' section, offering further thoughts about, or practical application of what you have been studying.

You may find it helpful to keep a journal to record your thoughts about your study, or to note items for prayer. Another way of using *Guidelines* is to meet with others to discuss the material, either regularly or occasionally.

Occasionally, you may read something in *Guidelines* that you find particularly challenging, even uncomfortable. This is inevitable in a series of notes which draws on a wide spectrum of contributors, and doesn't believe in ducking difficult issues. Indeed, we believe that *Guidelines* readers much prefer thought-provoking material to a bland diet that only confirms what they already think.

If you do disagree with a contributor, you may find it helpful to go through these three steps. First, think about why you feel uncomfortable. Perhaps this is an idea that is new to you, or you are not happy at the way something has been expressed. Or there may be something more substantial—you may feel that the writer is guilty of sweeping generalisation, factual error, theological or ethical misjudgment. Second, pray that God would use this disagreement to teach you more about his word and about yourself. Third, think about what you will do as a result of the disagreement. You might resolve to find out more about the issue, or write to the contributor or the editors of *Guidelines*. After all, we aim to be 'doers of the word', not just people who hold opinions about it.

Writers in this issue

Volker Rabens teaches New Testament at Ruhr-University Bochum, Germany. He is the author of *The Holy Spirit and Ethics in Paul: Transformation and Empowering for Religious-Ethical Life*.

Andrew Wingate was involved in theological education for 25 years in India and the UK. He moved to Leicester in 2000, and developed the St Philip's Centre for Study and Engagement in a Multi Faith Society. He is also Bishop's Inter Faith Adviser, and a Chaplain to The Queen.

Jane Williams read Theology at Cambridge University before going on to work in theological publishing and education. She now works as a Visiting Lecturer at King's College London, as a Lecturer at the St Paul's Theological Centre, and for Redemptorist Publications.

Jeremy Duff is a vicar in Widnes with a teaching and writing ministry, which has included posts at Liverpool Cathedral and within Oxford University. His writings include *Meeting Jesus: Human Responses to a Yearning God* (SPCK, 2006) and *The Elements of New Testament Greek* (CUP, 2005).

Henry Wansbrough OSB is a monk at Ampleforth Abbey in Yorkshire. He is Executive Secretary of the International Commission for Producing an English-Language Lectionary (ICPEL) for the Roman Catholic Church, and lectures frequently across the globe.

Justin Welby is Dean of Liverpool. Previously, as Canon of Coventry Cathedral, he was responsible for Coventry's international ministry of reconciliation. Justin is also the Personal and Ethical Adviser to the UK Association of Corporate Treasurers, and lectures extensively on ethics and finance.

Melissa Jackson recently completed her doctoral work at the University of Oxford. Her thesis was an examination of the intersection of comedy and feminist interpretation in several Old Testament stories. She is a lecturer in Old Testament and Hebrew at Baptist Theological Seminary, Richmond, Virginia, USA.

Chris Tilling is the New Testament Tutor at St Mellitus College and St Paul's Theological Centre, London. His present area of research concerns the apostle Paul's understanding of the identity of Christ.

Robert Mackley read history and theology at Cambridge University before ordination. Fr Robert is currently Assistant Chaplain and Research Student at Emmanuel College, Cambridge. He is a published church historian and a regular columnist and reviewer for the *Church Times*.

Further BRF reading for this issue

For more in-depth coverage of some of the passages in these Bible reading notes, we recommend the following titles:

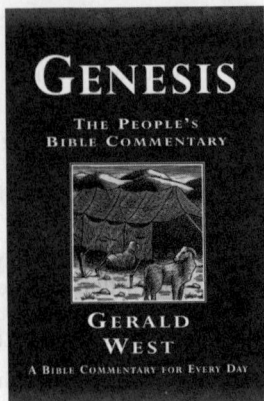

GENESIS

THE PEOPLE'S
BIBLE COMMENTARY

GERALD
WEST

A BIBLE COMMENTARY FOR EVERY DAY

978 1 84101 314 5, £8.99

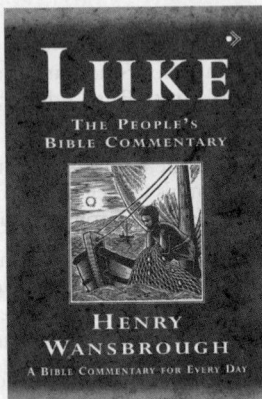

LUKE

THE PEOPLE'S
BIBLE COMMENTARY

HENRY
WANSBROUGH

A BIBLE COMMENTARY FOR EVERY DAY

978 1 84101 027 4, £7.99

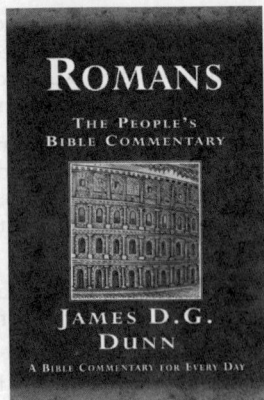

ROMANS

THE PEOPLE'S
BIBLE COMMENTARY

JAMES D.G.
DUNN

A BIBLE COMMENTARY FOR EVERY DAY

978 1 84101 082 3, £8.99

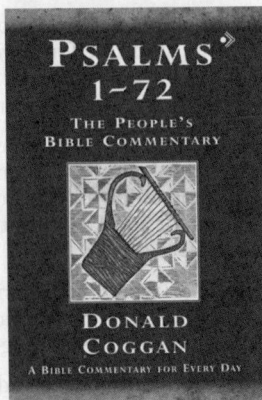

PSALMS
1–72

THE PEOPLE'S
BIBLE COMMENTARY

DONALD
COGGAN

A BIBLE COMMENTARY FOR EVERY DAY

978 1 84101 031 1, £8.99

The Editor writes…

New insights into familiar situations, words or ideas are precious. They are not always immediately welcome, for it can be uncomfortable to be disturbed, challenging to have to rethink. Nor is there a value in chasing after 'the new'. Nevertheless, without fresh insights, what was once meaningful, stimulating and life-giving can become dull and fade into the background. In this edition of *Guidelines* we look together at many familiar passages and ideas.

We begin with the second half of Ephesians, started last edition by Volker Rabens. Here we tackle some of the most fundamental questions of 'how to live', asked in the context of the uniting love of God. This same theme of 'how to live' continues when Andrew Wingate helps us consider 'Encountering people of other faiths'. As Andrew points out, this is in fact an age-old question, but one of great relevance in our age. Then Jane Williams leads us 'back to the beginning' to study again the very familiar but crucially important text of Genesis 1—11. From there we go to the last part, for now, of our study of Luke's Gospel with Jeremy Duff. Luke 10:17—13:35 contains familiar passages such as the good Samaritan, Martha and Mary, and the Lord's Prayer. Can God still speak to us through these?

Psalm 23 is probably the best-known biblical text after the Lord's Prayer. It is one of the passages that Henry Wansbrough guides us through in our next instalment of the Psalms. From there we tackle the issue of reconciliation, a word, as Justin Welby explains, 'from which the value is draining, as it loses its very deep roots and becomes an expression for a quick fix that stops an argument'. What fresh insight can God give us here? A different approach is then pursued by Melissa Jackson, who encourages us to see humour in the book of Esther—a more unusual method for biblical interpretation but one which is particularly suited to this unusual book. Then, guided by Chris Tilling, we come to the second part of Romans. Here Paul wrestles with the perennial issue of God's faithfulness, asking, 'If God's promises are fulfilled in Jesus, what of ethnic Israel?' Finally we come to Christmas, where Robert Mackley helps us see fresh insight into the familiar but awesome accounts of God coming among us.

As we read and study, assisted by our contributors in this edition, let us pray that God will give us new insights, challenge us and perhaps even disturb us.

The BRF Prayer

Almighty God,
you have taught us that your word is a lamp for our
feet and a light for our path. Help us, and all who
prayerfully read your word, to deepen our
fellowship with each other through your love. And
in so doing may we come to know you more fully,
love you more truly, and follow more faithfully in
the steps of your son Jesus Christ, who lives and
reigns with you and the Holy Spirit,
one God for evermore. Amen.

A Prayer for Remembrance

Heavenly Father, we commit ourselves to work in
penitence and faith for reconciliation between the
nations, that all people may, together, live in
freedom, justice and peace. We pray for all who in
bereavement, disability and pain continue to suffer
the consequences of fighting and terror. We
remember with thanksgiving and sorrow those
whose lives, in world wars and conflicts past and
present, have been given and taken away.

From An Order of Service for Remembrance Sunday,
Churches Together in Britain and Ireland 2005

Ephesians 4—6

We conclude our study of the letter to the Ephesians with the last three chapters, which are dedicated mainly to ethical guidance in the context of Paul's cosmic vision of the uniting love of God. Paul was a dreamer with a grand vision of the unity of the church, but also a realist who addressed the practical challenges of our life together. Only as we are grounded in and empowered by God's love will we be able to live in the unity that Christ brings.

Unless otherwise stated, quotations are taken from the New Revised Standard Version of the Bible.

1 Be what you are

Ephesians 4:1–16

The second part of Ephesians starts with an appeal—the first appeal in the letter. This says quite a bit about God and his dealings with us. Often we perceive God primarily as someone who wants something from us—our life, our time and, most of all, perfect behaviour. However, in this epistle, in which Paul unfolds the gospel and its implications without having to major on the specific problems of a particular church, the first half is fully occupied with what God did and does for us.

This emphasis on God's initiative in our lives continues in the second half of the epistle. Paul does not say, 'God has saved you, and now get your act together to live accordingly!' Rather, his ethical appeals are based on God's prior and continuous action. This approach starts right from the beginning of chapter 4, when Paul draws attention to the fact that it was God who called the Ephesians. It is reminiscent of how God created the world and 'called' (the same word is used in the Greek translation of Genesis 1) the different parts of creation by their names. God creates out of nothing, and now we can align ourselves in this creative act by 'being what we are'.

The same holds true for the practical ethical attitudes that Paul calls for in verse 2. They function to 'maintain the unity of the Spirit' (v. 3).

This re-emphasises the salvific reality that Paul talked about in chapter 2: God has reconciled the alienated groups of Jews and Gentiles. We don't have to create unity in the church, but we are called to maintain what is already there in the spiritual world. Paul thus returns to his grand vision of unity. He supports it by stressing the unitary nature of the central pillars of Christian faith: one body, one Spirit and so on (vv. 4–5). It culminates in the Father and the Son being 'above all and through all and in all' (v. 6; see v. 10). While Paul seems to understand this almost as a present reality in Ephesians, in 1 Corinthians 15 he prophesies of 'the end', when 'all things are subjected to [Christ]… so that God may be all in all' (vv. 24–28). It will mean the destruction of all forces of disunity and evil. What a glorious future to look ahead to!

2 Living in accordance with the new creation

Ephesians 4:17–24

In the previous section, Paul formulated positively what it means to live as a Christian. Gentleness, patience and love are central to this lifestyle (4:2). Also, building one another up through exercising spiritual gifts plays a role (4:7–13). Now Paul describes what is not characteristic of Christian life, and does so by means of a somewhat stereotyped depiction of Gentile life. Interestingly, this depiction does not start with moral shortcomings. Rather, it starts with alienation from God. The lack of relationship with God, actively turning a hard heart on him, has had multiple effects in their lives. The progression is reminiscent of that in Romans 1:18–32. In Ephesians 4, the major consequence is the loss of all sensitivity (v. 19). This formulation implies that sensitivity had been there before—as a part of being created in God's image (Genesis 1:27). The good news for Christians is that what once was lost has now been found: they are '[re]created according to the likeness of God in true righteousness and holiness' (v. 24).

However, this re-creation does not bring an instant new self, having no continuity with our 'old' self. For example, everyone has different habits—some of them helpful, some of them not so helpful. These habits, as well as everything else in us, need to be brought into congruence with 'the way [we] learned Christ' (v. 20). Jesus embodies the truth, and if we wish to

8

live in it we need to put off our 'former way of life' and embrace a life like his. We put off a lifestyle characterised by 'deceitful desires' (v. 22, NIV), desires that constantly make promises but never fully satisfy, that consume but rarely fulfil.

The old humanity is thus marked by the twilight of deceitful, corrupting desires; the antidote is constant renewal in the full light of the truth set out by Paul thus far. As we have just seen, this truth is relational and not propositional, which means that it has to do with how we 'learned Christ'. It is in our encounters with Jesus that we learn what this new humanity looks like.

What could it mean for you today to (continue to) put on the new humanity?

3 Love and justice

Ephesians 4:25—5:20

Paul continues with a number of ethical guidelines, the majority of which concern interpersonal relationships. In this text, Paul exhibits a spectrum of thought that is often understood as inconsistent in itself. On one side, he stresses truth and justice, and on the other side he speaks up for grace and forgiveness. Paul starts off by emphasising the value of truth in our talking with one another. The reason for this is weighty: we are members of one another. We belong so intimately to one another that we cannot but be fully truthful. However, this truthfulness is not in tension with love. In 4:32—5:2, Paul explains how love and forgiveness can and should be characteristic of our attitude towards others, namely by imitating God's love of us. God's love of us enables us to love others.

This love is also the basis of Paul's instruction to let go of our anger before the sun goes down (4:26). When we are angry with another person, Paul calls us not to sin. Sinning would mean taking revenge ourselves. However, Paul does not say that being angry about an injustice done to us is wrong. In line with his emphasis on justice, he takes account of the fact that we are angry in such situations. He literally says 'be angry...' (imperative). The forgiveness to which he encourages us is not 'cheap' or superficial. He explains that we should forgive one another 'as God in Christ has forgiven you' (v. 32). Because God is a God of love and justice, Christ has died for us. Death is the ultimate revenge for all the injustice done to ourselves and others in this world. God himself has stepped in and, in Jesus Christ, has died this death.

As God is interested in justice, forgiving does not mean playing down what has been done to us. Paul is speaking here in the style of ancient proverbial wisdom. His exhortation not to let the sun go down over our anger is therefore not a law carved in stone. It is good advice for everyday dealings in the family and among our neighbours. However, it is clearly not applicable to every kind of deed that evokes and deserves anger—for example, sexual exploitation, racial persecution or other kinds of abuse that stem from systematic evil. Depending on how severe the offence was, forgiving can mean a (life)long process of handing it over to the God of justice and love.

4 Love and respect

Ephesians 5:21–33

Paul's ethical teaching is very practical. Now he shares his thoughts about the Christian household. Some translations start a new section here with verse 22, but that is a mistake, because this verse is lacking a verb. 'Be subject' is used only in the preceding verse, and is then carried forward to verse 22. This means that the submission of the wife needs to be comprehended in the context of mutual submission. Husband and wife are called to submit to one another out of reverence for Christ. However, as both Paul and his churches live in a patriarchal society, mutual submission in marriage is spelled out in terms of the husband loving the wife (vv. 25–30) and the wife respecting the husband (vv. 22–24; see the summary in v. 33). Because of this aspect of mutuality and the amount of space given to the exhortation of the husband to love his wife (five verses), Paul's instructions can be described as 'love-patriarchalism'.

Paul seems not to intend to revolutionise his society by turning the hierarchical household model on its head, but he nonetheless transforms it from within. A wife's submission would have been naturally expected in the ancient world, especially as the wife could have been as much as 15 years younger than her husband and the marriage would have been arranged. Consequently, in the first-century context, this submission can be seen as appropriate, but the element of authority is not inherent for all time. Paul is indicating the way wives should be submissive within a society where such behaviour is expected, just as he can also tell slaves how they are to be obedient in the slave–master relationship; in both cases he bases it on the relationship to Christ. However, the wife is not her husband's body (as verse 28 makes clear), and the Christ–church relationship is an analogy or pattern, not a ground for the wife's submission.

In this text, Paul stays within the framework of patriarchalism but transforms it from within by drawing attention to Christ's self-giving love as the norm. Elsewhere, though, he is more explicitly countercultural—for example, when he says that 'there is no longer slave or free, there is no longer male and female; for all of you are one in Christ Jesus' (Galatians 3:28). We will turn to the implication of this maxim in the next section.

5 Love and work

Ephesians 6:1–9

In the second part of the household instructions, Paul addresses the relationships of parents and children and of masters and slaves. Paul's guidance for the first group is relatively straightforward to transfer to today's context (though bearing in mind that, in the ancient world, the obedience of children continued to a more advanced age; in today's West, Christians would teach children to develop independence of their parents and learn to make their own decisions wisely and 'in the Lord'). However, with regard to the second group, it has been generally accepted since the abolition of the slave trade that slavery is morally wrong. Did Paul have a different set of values?

To begin with, it is important to see that Paul does not just accept the conventions of slavery but challenges key aspects of them. This comes to the fore when he requires masters to treat their slaves in the 'same' way as he has instructed the slaves to behave (v. 9a). This implies that masters are 'subject' to their slaves (see 5:21). Generally speaking, Paul did not overturn the cultural convention of slavery, which was essential to the smooth running of an ancient economy. However, in the long run, the equality before God (v. 9) that Paul so pointedly formulated in Galatians 3:28

has to transform the way we relate to one another in church and society. Throughout church history, Christians have applied the central message of the gospel to social and ethical issues afresh, as new situations and societal structures have arisen. So, while the recognition that slavery is incompatible with Christian faith goes beyond the explicit teaching of scripture, it is nonetheless fully scriptural, for slavery is inconsistent with the biblical understanding of humanity in creation and redemption.

We can conclude that Paul's household teaching accepted the given structures but implicitly challenged them in the direction of greater equality. The full force of Galatians 3:28 can be applied to our churches today as we live in a more egalitarian society, which does not depend on the subordination of women and slaves. Requiring such subordination today would mean moving in the opposite direction of that taken by Paul.

What issues in our society come to your mind (in relation to family, work and other everyday situations) for which we need a fresh application of the values of the gospel?

6 Holding firm to the new reality

Ephesians 6:10–24

Paul was not a triumphalist. While the predominant message of this letter is that Christ sits on the throne (1:20–21) and that his kingdom is coming on earth, Paul is also clear that Christ's kingdom has not fully come, and that it is hence only in a certain sense that Christ sits on the throne (de jure, not fully de facto). On earth, we have evil days. Darkness is very present (vv. 12–13). God's will may be done, not done, ignored or even opposed. This is the spectrum within which we live. God has committed himself to giving a certain amount of freedom to humankind, which means that the bad things that happen generally result from the bad choices of human beings—directly or indirectly (indirectly because the dynamics of this present darkness, as human suffering, are the result of humankind's general alienation from God).

However, our text also mentions actual forces of evil, which belong to Paul's concept of 'present darkness' (v. 12). How do these forces intend to influence our lives, and how can we resist?

The main endeavour of the dark forces is to take away something that is already there. Throughout the letter, Paul has majored on the cosmic reconciliation achieved by Christ, but this 'gospel of peace' (v. 15) is at risk. The opponent forces are interested to see us not maintaining the unity of the Spirit, attaining to maturity in Christ, dealing with anger, cultivating edifying talk, loving in marriage and so on. On the other hand, it is exactly through putting these godly attitudes and actions into practice that we can 'stand against the wiles of the devil' (v. 11; compare 4:26–27). In this way we are able to stand in the strength of God's power (1:19–20).

In fact, our 'spiritual armour' also turns out to be a mixture of God's very own (see Isaiah 59:17) with that of his Messiah (Isaiah 11:4–5). It enables us to hold on to our strong position. Paul's exhortation is not preparing us, like soldiers, to make a moving attack (note that the Roman soldier's key attack weapons, the twin javelins, are missing), but to stand firm (vv. 11, 13–14). We hold the crown of the hill, as it were, and the enemy must weary itself in constant uphill attack.

Let us 'pray in the Spirit' (v. 18) in order to fathom and hold firm to the new reality of God's power and his gospel of peace.

Guidelines

In the second part of the epistle, Paul has unfolded what his cosmic vision of the uniting love of God means for everyday living. Knowing the love of Christ that surpasses knowledge (3:19) and being grounded in it (3:17) is a life-transforming experience. Paul has opened a number of pathways for this love to flow into the context that the Ephesian churches faced. The majority of his teaching concerns interpersonal relationships, and this gets as practical as spelling out what following Christ's way of love actually means for living in family and work structures.

The progression of thought of the letter can be summarised in terms of the three verbs 'sit', 'walk' and 'stand'. The first part of the letter dealt with Christian identity in terms of status and position. Our participation in Christ's victory over the powers is expressed most strikingly in the assertion that we have been seated with Christ in the heavenly realms (2:6). The second part of the letter, with its repeated use of the verb 'to walk' in all its sections, encourages us to live out our status and calling in the world. The concluding exhortation to 'stand' combines both of these earlier emphases in its call to maintain and appropriate our position of strength and victory as we live out our lives in the world, in the face of opposing evil cosmic powers.

At the very end of the letter, Paul comes back to the focal points of his message and appeal. He wishes his readers peace, love and faith (6:23). Peace, which is the consequence of the cosmic reconciliation and God's great love, has had a grand exposition in the epistle. Faith, in this letter, is the radical openness to God that allows Christ's full indwelling and brings a deeper grasp of his unfathomable love (see 3:17). By specifying all three as coming from the Father and the Lord Jesus Christ (6:23), Paul shows how much his ethics is grounded in the first half of his letter and its emphasis on what God has done and continues to do.

Let us 'sit' to receive God's peace, love and faith(fulness) so that we are able to 'walk' and 'stand' in it, too.

FURTHER READING

J.D.G. Dunn, 'Ephesians', in J. Barton and J. Muddiman (eds.), *The Oxford Bible Commentary* (OUP, 2001), pp. 1165–79.

Andrew T. Lincoln, *Ephesians* (WBC 42) (Word, 1990).

I. Howard Marshall, 'Mutual Love and Submission in Marriage: Colossians 3:18–19 and Ephesians 5:21–33', in R.W. Pierce, R.M. Groothuis and G.D. Fee (eds.), *Discovering Biblical Equality: Complementarity without Hierarchy* (IVP, 2005), pp. 186–204.

Max Turner, 'Ephesians', in D.A. Carson, R.T. France, J.A. Motyer and G.J. Wenham (eds.), *New Bible Commentary: 21st Century Edition* (IVP, 1994), pp. 1222–44.

Encountering people of other faiths

Both Old and New Testaments were born out of a multi-faith world. They are the record of a range of writers who interacted with the context of their time, and that context was multi-cultural, multi-ethnic and multi-faith. How were the Jewish people, who believed they had been chosen by the One God, to relate to those who had no such monotheistic faith? How were they to preserve the integrity of that faith as a minority community battling continuously for their survival, and to maintain the purity of their worship? How were they to affirm the ethic which was a consequence of their calling—to care for the stranger, the widow, the orphan and the poor—against the pressures of power and the pressures of survival? And what of the world before they became conscious of themselves as a chosen people? What of the creation of the world, the early history of humankind and the origin of evil—how were they to think of these questions in a world of diverse faiths, histories and philosophies?

Jesus inherited such a world, in which his people were caught within the power-pressures of their position as a small and remote province of the Roman Empire. He was, of course, born a Jew and he died a Jew, as did all his disciples, but he was convinced that his message of the kingdom of God was for all people, of whatever culture and ethnic background.

The greatest evangelist of Jesus incarnated three such backgrounds within his person. Paul was a Jew of Jews, a Roman citizen, and a Greek in culture. He became critical in struggling with the question of how to relate the deeply transforming good news of God 'in Christ... reconciling the world to himself' (2 Corinthians 5:19)—including 'those who were far off and those who were near' (see Ephesians 2:17)—to the Jewish tradition into which the Christian faith had first been born. So also the Gospel writers, as they affirmed such universality within the diversity of their intended readership: they wrote both for those within the infant churches and those outside, to whom they communicated the person of Jesus Christ and his message of the universality of God's love. At the same time, the New Testament letter writers faced the dilemmas of how to guide the recipients of their letters to practise their new faith where they lived, as Christian small minorities. Another challenge was how to give testimony to the mystery of Jesus—the extraordinary (and, for his fellow Jews at least, blasphemous) message that he was 'the word made flesh' (John 1:14), and that his death and resurrection were of saving significance, 'a stumbling block to Jews, and foolishness to Gentiles' (1 Corinthians 1:23).

We begin with four passages from the Hebrew Bible, followed by eight passages from the Gospels and epistles. A word to begin with from the great missionary theologian, Max Warren, written 50 years ago, but as fresh now as when first written:

'Our first task in approaching another people, another culture, is to take off our shoes, for the place we are approaching is holy. Else we may find our selves treading on men's dreams... We have to try and sit where they sit, to enter sympathetically into the pains and griefs and joys of their history, and see how those pains and griefs and joys have determined the premises of their argument. We have, in a word, to be "present" with them.' (Max Warren, preface to Kenneth Cragg, *Sandals at the Mosque*, SCM, 1959, p. 9)

Unless otherwise stated, quotations are taken from the New Revised Standard Version.

1 Universal challenges

Genesis 3

The first eleven chapters of the Hebrew Bible are about the whole of humankind—indeed, the whole of creation. All are created by the One God through his Spirit, for there is only one God. Humanity is created good, and Genesis 3 is written to address the question, 'Why, then, do human beings universally sin?' We all know the experience of Paul, summarised in Romans 7:19: 'For I do not do the good I want but the evil I do not want is what I do.' The result of Adam and Eve's sin is the universality of death. Also affirmed here is human responsibility. We cannot hide permanently behind the tree (v. 8); we have to own what we do. The sin is to have defied God and claimed autonomy from God in making moral choices.

Different religions have their various responses to these universal questions about creation, evil and death. Genesis 3 is the Judeo-Christian version, in which it is a matter of human choice, of free will being exercised

(v. 6). The Qur'an has a similar story, but with significant differences. Many Christians, perhaps most, hold that these passages are 'myths', and all the richer for that: they are stories with profundity of meaning. Muslims normally hold to a literal interpretation of the account, as Christian so-called 'creationists' do. However, Muslims also hold that Adam did not 'sin' but made a mistake out of ignorance. He is able to repent and the status quo may be restored. He is a prophet, and prophets cannot sin. Hence, there is no 'original sin' in Islam.

For Hindus and Buddhists, it is a question of maya—not seeing rightly. Ignorance must be replaced by spiritual knowledge, seeing rightly. In the Judeo-Christian tradition, we may see 'rightly' but still make the wrong choice, out of the weakness of our will power.

In Genesis 1:26, the ecological question is addressed. Human beings have responsibility for the goodness of creation, not licence to use it as they please. There are few more contemporary challenges than this, and all faiths have to come together, with those of no religious faith, if we are to make any impact before we destroy God's good earth through exploitation. As the opening chapters of Genesis develop, we see the consequences of evil culminating in the story of Noah. In chapter 9, we experience God's universal covenant with all, as expressed to Noah. All are embraced by this promise of God, as signalled by the rainbow. God's ultimate love is without boundaries and is not limited to either Jewish or Christian people. He will not destroy the earth, but humanity is on the road to doing so, if we do not repent and act radically.

2 Abraham, Sarah and Hagar

Genesis 21:8–20

Abraham is the great unifying figure for Jews, Christians and Muslims. He is seen as the father of three faiths, because he responded to the Lord's calling to leave the safety of his land (in present-day Iraq) to spread the blessing of the God to all nations (Genesis 12:1–3).

In Genesis 21, we find one of the many unexpected gems of the Old Testament. It is the line from Sarah, the 'legitimate' wife of Abraham, that is normally heralded in Judeo-Christian tradition. God is seen to work through that line to give the land of Canaan in perpetuity, as well as the responsibility for fulfilling the covenant as God's people. But here, Sarah shows her unsavoury side (v. 10). When she sees her own son Isaac playing with the older boy Ishmael, also Abraham's son through Hagar the slave woman, she persuades Abraham to cast out Hagar and Ishmael.

Abraham shows compassion in the way he does this, but away they are sent. Then follows the remarkable passage in which the despised Hagar and her son are made the direct recipients of God's loving care (vv. 17–19). A great nation will descend through Ishmael, and not just one through Isaac (v. 13)—a promise that begins to be fulfilled in 25:12–18, through the Arabian tribes. In the Qur'an, it is Hagar and Ishmael who take the prime place. The key story of the sacrifice of Isaac (Genesis 22) is replaced by the proposed sacrifice of Ishmael, which is celebrated in one of the two great Muslim Eid festivals.

Would that all three Abrahamic faiths could have the openness to recognise that the descendants of both Hagar and Sarah were blessed by God; and that today's descendants from Abraham—Jews, Christians and Muslims—could feel more of the distress of Abraham when they conflict with each other. Would that they could 'play' together, like the children Ishmael and Isaac, rather than war with each other. In Britain, the Three Faiths Forum is working to this aim, as are local groups such as the 'Family of Abraham' group in Leicester. Perhaps cricket and football matches between Christians and Muslims, as seen in Leicester and other cities, are a tangible way of 'playing together'? What can we do in our own locality to enable understanding between Abrahamic faiths? There are few more urgent challenges internationally, of course, but small is beautiful and we can begin where we are.

3 The power of repentance

Jonah 3—4

This is an extraordinary passage to find in the Hebrew Bible. A late Jewish prophet is taught a deeply subversive lesson. The people of the wicked city of Nineveh, capital of the empire of Assyria, which had harmed Jews much over three centuries, are the recipients not of God's revengeful justice but of his mercy. All they do is repent when they hear Jonah's message. But Jonah is so very human as he displays his anger that they have received God's forgiveness. He himself affirms the supremacy of God's love and mercy (4:2), but, when it comes to these particular people, it is very different. He even feels more for the plant that has given him shade than for the vast human population of Nineveh and their cattle.

This is a powerful story with a profound challenge. Jonah was forced to learn that God's love is universal and even the wickedest of people may repent. Are we ready for the spiritual challenge of the way some people of other faiths give us lessons in humility before God? Are we willing to accept that God's mercy and, indeed, salvific will are potentially universal in scope, reaching to those who submit to him in repentance? Why are we afraid of the breadth of the message of this small book? As the hymn writer says, 'We make his love too narrow by false limits of our own, and we magnify his strictness with a zeal he will not own' (F.W. Faber, 'There's a wideness in God's mercy').

Perhaps there is an anticipation here of the challenge inherent in the stories of the Canaanite woman (Matthew 15:21–28), the faithful centurion (Matthew 8:5–13) and the repentant thief who was crucified next to Jesus (Luke 23:39–43). Jonah's attitude can be likened also to the righteous anger of the elder son in the story of the prodigal son (Luke 15:11–32). Can we appreciate the demonstration of repentance before God seen in certain people of other faiths whom we know? Are we prepared to open our hearts to them, as God did to the people of Nineveh?

4 Interfaith marriage

Nehemiah 13:23–27; Ruth 1:5–18

The closest form of interfaith encounter is through mixed-faith marriages or families. The major strand of the Old Testament is adamantly against interfaith marriage. We see it explicitly forbidden in Deuteronomy 7:3–4. At that time, the supreme task was to preserve the faith as a small minority in an alien land, and so it has continued in the Jewish diaspora. It was about race and ethnicity as much as about faith, and, until today, within Orthodox Judaism, a female who marries out brings to an end the Jewish connection. The prohibition was at its most hostile with the return from exile, as recorded in Ezra 9 and Nehemiah 13:23–30. Intermarriage was an abomination and apostasy, and even involved speaking the language of the pagan!

Against this there is little in the Old Testament, but standing out as an exception is the book of Ruth. Ruth was a Moabite, married to a Jew, who died. She then made an unforgettable commitment to her Jewish mother-in-law Naomi, 'Your people shall be my people, and your God my God' (1:16). Ruth went with Naomi to Bethlehem, where she married Boaz, Naomi's dead husband's relative. Through Ruth's line came David, Jesse and eventually Jesus.

The New Testament has little to say on this theme. Paul writes against early Christians being yoked together with 'unbelievers' (2 Corinthians 6:14), but in 1 Corinthians 7:12–16 he gives the hope that an unbelieving spouse may be sanctified by the believing partner. In multi-faith Britain, interfaith marriage is increasing. It can be deeply sacramental and the deepest example of dialogue, or it can be full of pitfalls, which may be about faith, culture or ethnicity. As Christians, we may not wish for a mixed-faith partnership for our children, but, when it happens, we should welcome the partner of another faith. We should show the kind of love highlighted in 1 Corinthians 13 and, as with any marriage, provide the support needed to help the couple grow closer. We should also remember that, as in biblical times, marriage is about the uniting of two extended families, and so the wider family is inevitably involved.

5 The surprise of encounter

John 4:4–27

The question is often asked, 'Why interfaith dialogue, and why are Christians the ones who normally start it?' Why do we have to go to them, to their leaders, temples and mosques? But this is precisely what Jesus did in this unforgettable passage. He went to the well of Jacob, the well used by the Samaritan village. His disciples were surprised about where he had gone (v. 27), as is the case for many congregation members who mutter if their minister sees it as a priority to meet people of other faiths.

At the well, Jesus begins the dialogue not with theology but by asking for something very tangible—a drink of water. In doing this, he crosses four barriers—those of gender, culture (high caste and 'untouchable'), faith (Samaritans were heretics, who only accepted the five books of Moses), and morality (the woman has had five husbands and is now cohabiting). He is ready to receive across all these divides, and receiving is more difficult than giving. The result is a vigorous encounter, which ends with the woman learning the source of living water and bringing many of her fellow villagers to faith. Jesus is led to enunciate a thought that is so enabling for interfaith relations—that God is Spirit, and that true worship is not about place but about spirit and truth. Can true worship take place in a mosque, or Sikh Gurdwara, or Hindu home?

Have we got the courage to cross such barriers? Do we have confidence that 'perfect love casts out all fear' (1 John 4:18)? Can we see God as the 'go-between God' (as memorably named by John Taylor)—the third person in the encounter between people of faith? I named a book that I wrote *Encounter in the Spirit* (WCC, 1991). This was an account of interfaith dialogue between Christians and Muslims in Birmingham over four years, explaining what I had learnt from it about my own faith as well as the faith of the other. Rowan Williams has said this: 'We have to see how very other our universes are; and only then do we find dialogue a surprise and a joy, as we also discover where and how we can still talk about what matters most—holiness, being at peace and what truly is' (from a lecture given at Birmingham University, 11 June 2003; full lecture available on the Archbishop's website: www.archbishopofcanterbury.org/2196).

6 The breadth of God's love

Luke 4:16–30

This so-called 'Nazareth manifesto' led to an attempt to lynch Jesus (v. 29). It was not because he had dared to claim, in his home synagogue, that he fulfilled Isaiah 61 (though, notably, he did not include the message of vengeance that appears in Isaiah 61:2). That was challenging in itself. But he also asserted, in the Lukan account, that God took special healing care of the Canaanite widow in Sidon, and Naaman the Syrian, ahead of Jews suffering from famine or leprosy.

These passages have much to say about narrowness of vision with regard to God's love. The people of Nazareth could not bear to hear the message that God's love extended beyond their own people (compare the story of Jonah). Do we, as Christians, often feel that we have privileges because we are Christians? The work of Christian Aid is radically opposed to such a restrictive view. Aid is given to people regardless of their faith, but this is not always appreciated by local churches in recipient contexts. The same response can be found in the UK, where Christian projects reach out to asylum seekers, the majority of whom are Muslims, when there are so many needy 'of our own'. More positively, Islamic Relief works closely with Christian Aid in several places, having learnt to share the vision that care should not be limited to Muslims. A major Hindu temple in Leicester gives a considerable donation each Christian Aid week to the local church, because they are impressed by the way aid is given, regardless of faith.

The story of Naaman shows how the Syrian commander healed of leprosy by Elisha came to faith in Yahweh, but was still allowed to go through the rituals of his ancestral faith in his master's temple of Rimmon, the god of storm and war (2 Kings 5:18–19a). Do we put pressure upon the convert to be 'pure' and to give up family religious practices, according to our timing, not when the convert feels ready? Today some of the Naamans of our world are known as 'secret Christians', and there are many such in our society, whether Hindu, Sikh or Muslim. Others are open Christians but feel they should participate in family rituals for birth, marriage and death. Others will decide to have a clean break. This can lead to hurt or conflict and can prevent Christian witness to family and the former community.

Guidelines

It is important to begin with Genesis, with the fundamental religious challenges that this book brings to human thinking. These challenges are to all of us, whatever religious label we carry, or even if we are humanistic in our worldview. Genesis 21 shows how God's care extends beyond the Jewish line on which the rest of the Hebrew scriptures are focused.

The remaining four passages we have read this week bring out the struggle involved in accepting that God's love is limitless, as God longs to embrace all humanity. The barriers to this acceptance are human limitations—our wish to make rules that include people 'like us' and to erect walls against that breadth of love. The Gospel passages from John and Luke provide glimpses of how Jesus challenged those barriers, and show how the people in his own home town of Nazareth, and even his own disciples, did not like this at all. We are challenged to think about how we react today to the same subversive message about God's love.

1 How to enter eternal life

Luke 10:25–37

The power of this parable is often blunted by over-familiarity. We are to be like the good Samaritan, yes, and this is central to Christian ethics. We are not to pass by on the other side when someone is in serious need of help. Someone who is 'untouchable' can show us the way, as he or she sees the priority of compassion, when so-called religious people do not stop. Are we willing to give more than the bare minimum, as the Samaritan did at the inn (v. 35)?

More radically, though, are we willing not just to give but also to receive from the Samaritans of our time, be they asylum seekers, those who are HIV-positive or others on the margins? What about people of other faiths? I think of an elderly and lonely member of our congregation who brings her Sikh neighbour to church. She tells with gratitude of how she received a full Christmas meal, cooked 'as she knows it' from this Sikh family next door. I think of a neighbour whose husband was very ill. When he was returning from hospital, she could not get him from the car to his bed in the house. She tells how two Muslims, one an Imam, stopped on their way to the mosque and spent time lifting him into the house, making him comfortable and asking if she had any other needs, before going on late to their prayers. Her telling this story was a powerful witness in our Muslim-majority area.

Even more radically, this parable is told to illustrate to the 'expert in the law' (v. 25, NIV) what is necessary to enter eternal life. Is the Samaritan just an illustration of good action or, without expecting it, could he find himself inheriting eternal life? What about the Sikh family mentioned above? Might they enter heaven before me, a Christian priest with three degrees that prove my learnedness, if I ignore those in need because my church duties are so important? How wide are the gates of heaven?

2 True prayer?

Luke 18:9–14

St Philip's Church, Leicester, 100 years old, is on one side of the road; exactly opposite is Masjid Umar, an impressively built ten-year-old mosque. This mosque is undeniably a place of prayer. Attendances on Fridays are into four figures; every lunch time or evening, attendance is 200–300. In Ramadan this number increases considerably, especially in the last ten days, when a number of Muslims stay on retreat. I live nearby, and an elderly neighbour, a former railwayman, tells me that he is glad to have retired so that he can pray five times a day without difficulty. I see him making the short walk to the mosque, in the summer, from 4am until late in the evening. What does he go to do? To pray the simple prayer of the tax collector in this passage in Luke's Gospel, 'God, be merciful to me, a sinner' (v. 13). This sums up the spirit of Muslim *salat* (the formal required prayers). Can I say, with Jesus here, that my neighbour comes home 'justified'—the same word in Luke as 'saved'?

What can we say of the equality shown in the rows at Muslim prayer, shoulder touching shoulder? Can I learn something for our church congregations, in which people often sit far apart from each other? Muslims believe that their bodily posture in prayer is following the prophet's example. We often find it difficult to pray on our knees, though we were told that at the name of Jesus every knee shall bow (Philippians 2:10). Even more challengingly, what do we make of the Hindu elderly women who spend much of the day in a Hindu temple, singing Sanskrit or Gujarati bhajans (chants), in praise of their God, be it Siva or Rama? Or those who are part of the ISKON ('Hare Krishna') movement, with their daily devotion to Krishna, whom they see as the one God?

Of course, we believe that praying in the name of Jesus adds a dimension of deep significance and closeness—and I see that this mosque has no place for women to pray. Turkish Muslim women have come to church to pray, where they feel at home. Can the mosque learn something from this?

Here are two prayers of repentance from other faiths, for reflection. Tukaram, an Indian peasant in the 17th century, prayed: 'As a child that has lost its mother, so am I troubled, my heart is seared with sore anguish: O merciful God, thou knowest my need, come, save me, and show me thy love.' An Arabic prayer goes, 'It is glory enough for me that I should be your servant; it is grace enough for me that you should be my Lord.'

3 A proof text?

John 14:1–8

John 14:6 is often used like the proof in the geometry problems that schoolchildren used to be required to learn. QED: there is no more argument needed; there is just one way to God, one way to salvation, and all other religions are ruled out *a priori*. We cannot avoid tackling this text; indeed, it is deeply rich with its oft-quoted words, 'I am the way, and the truth, and the life', and the seemingly exclusive words that follow: 'No one comes to the Father except through me.'

But we should note that the verse does not say, 'No one comes to God…'. Clearly a way had been revealed to the Jewish people: such is the point of the pivotal calling of Abraham in Genesis 12. Jesus is talking here of the intimate relationship of the disciple, that he or she can call God *abba*, as privileged in the Lord's Prayer. A well-known Sikh convert sees this as his conversion text. He knew God in Sikhism, from his mother, but knowing God in Christ adds a life-giving dimension. Moreover, the Jesus here is the Christ of the Fourth Gospel, the one who is the Word through whom all are created (1:3), the one who brings life and light and truth (1:1–18). He said in 8:58, 'Before Abraham was, I am.' In this sense, there is no other way, because Christ is the self-revelation of God, and the presence of God, for all times and places. What is added in Jesus is not knowledge of God but fullness of relationship, as found between Jesus and his disciples.

A further key point is the context of 14:6. It is in answer to Simon Peter's question, 'Lord, where are you going?' (13:36), and Thomas' follow-on, 'How can we know the way?' (14:5). The way is that of John 13, the way of lowest servanthood, the washing of each other's feet. What follows is the way of the cross, where all except the beloved disciple run away. This is no comfy, exclusivist salvation text. Ultimately, though, 'in my Father's house are many rooms' (14:2, NIV). Can the love of God not open rooms for at least some of those who faithfully worship God in their own traditions, and love their neighbour? What 14:6 suggests is that such a room can only be opened through the Logos of God. John is not thinking here explicitly of other faiths: indeed, Islam and Sikhism were not yet born, and Hinduism was beyond his knowledge. The passage is addressed to believers or potential believers of the time, assuring them that they can know God in this intimate way in Christ.

4 Appropriate evangelism

Acts 17:16–33

Paul's encounter with these philosophers in Athens can be compared with Jesus' dialogue with the Samaritan woman (see last week's notes on John 4). What is in question here is not the sincerity of their beliefs—they were 'devout' (v. 17)—but the limitations of what they believe. Nevertheless, Paul goes to where they are secure, and engages with the philosophers on their terms. The Epicureans followed the teaching of Epicurus (born in Athens in 342BC), for whom the supreme value was pleasure, but only if their actions did not harm the people around them. Stoicism (founded by Zeno in 278BC) taught that its followers were to bear with equanimity whatever befell them, good or bad: 'whatever will be will be'. Clearly there are many modern followers of both, even if they do not bear the names.

Paul affirms what he can in the Athenians' scriptures and acknowledges their honest religious searching, with their altar 'To an unknown god'. He gives content to this aspiration. He begins with teaching about creation and, strikingly, the longing for God found in all humanity. He then makes known the unknown, without mentioning the name of Jesus, but rather setting out the radical action taken by God in raising from the dead 'the man he appointed' as judge, and the need for repentance. The message is clear, but it is offered in ways the listener can comprehend, if not accept. In Acts, Paul uses different ways to address his fellow Jews. In speaking of Jesus with Hindus, we can perhaps use this passage as a model; with Muslims it will be rather different, given their fiercely monotheistic faith and their affirmation of Jesus as a prophet. How do we show appreciation of this, but also explain why we believe that he is 'more than a prophet'? The message will be divisive, but so it is also in verse 32. Some in Athens became believers, as indeed do some Hindus, Sikhs and Muslims. What converts them is usually an encounter with Jesus rather than coming to a belief in God, which is usually already present. So it was with Paul's conversion (Acts 9).

5 Food sacrificed to idols

1 Corinthians 8:1–13; 10:23–31

These chapters represent a fine example of how Paul links practicality with theology. Engagement is followed by reflection. These passages have become particularly relevant in Britain in recent years, which have seen the opening of more than 150 Hindu temples, with their numerous 'idols' ('deities', 'images', 'representations', 'symbols'—various words are used; I have even heard 'angels'). Is the holy book, the Guru Granth Sahib, made de facto into an idol in a Sikh Gurdwara? It is placed in the centre of the worship hall, and the devout fall prostrate before it.

Paul's advice to Corinthian Christians can be extrapolated to our context, when visitors to temples or guests in Hindu homes are offered food blessed by a priest before idols or deities. Paul's advice is sound: if love demands (8:1), eat; for, if idols are nothing, it will do you no harm. But consider those who are with you: they can make their own mind up, and, if they are offended by your eating, abstain.

Indian Christians will usually find my eating confusing, since they or their ancestors often suffered for their decision to convert. The William Carey Memorial Baptist Church became a temple in the 1970s, and is now the leading temple in Leicester. This is deeply upsetting to Protestant Indian Christians, since Carey, who went from Leicester to Bengal and began the Baptist mission, is a legend for them. Hindus, however, deeply respect the building's holy origins.

As a minister, my eating can put pressure on lay people to eat, and afterwards they may feel bad. (If you are in a similar situation, always prepare a group beforehand for the experience.) But underneath there remains the theological principle that there is one God only, and these idols are nothing. The challenge is to consider whether the Hindus who appear to worship idols are in fact worshipping the one God beyond, as most will affirm. Challenge comes, too, when Hindus or Sikhs come to our Eucharist. What do we do when they hold out their hands for bread? The priority of love comes to the fore, I believe, at least on a one-off occasion.

6 Commending the gospel

Colossians 4:2–6

There is much wisdom in these verses, written by Paul from prison. Prayer should be at the heart of sensitive evangelism (v. 2), and such prayer should include thanksgiving. Why should people be attracted to a faith that appears full of gloom rather than joy? This is to be remembered as we prepare prayers for worship. The introduction to the Intercessions in the Anglican Communion service used to say, 'Let us pray for the church and for the world, *and let us thank God for his goodness*' (ASB, sadly omitted from *Common Worship*). Followers of other faiths know that Christians are full of good works, but where do they see Christians as people of prayer? Why follow a faith whose adherents seem often to be defensive or apologetic?

We need to wait for God to open a door for our testimony, which is to be about the mystery of Christ, not about peripheral things. The message is to be simple but not simplistic. The outsider—for our purposes, the person of another faith—is owed as much. Remember that kairos times of encounter come rarely, and we must make the most of them. Grace and kindness should go with salt and sharpness. We are to 'speak the truth in love' (Ephesians 4:15). There is no time for waffle or complication. Each person is different and each faith is different; our response should be phrased accordingly (v. 6). I was challenged by a close Muslim friend, 'We have talked about so many things, but we don't talk about the heart of our faiths. Tell me in five minutes, simply, without theological jargon, what is the centre of what you live by?' How would you answer this Muslim? And how would you to speak to a Hindu, Sikh or Jew who asked the same question? 'Your response will depend upon the questioner' would be the advice of Paul, but what should be consistent are grace, kindness, salt and sharpness.

Guidelines

The church has always lived in a multi-faith world. As it became politically triumphant, it paid scant attention to this situation, but in the 'mission fields' the reality of how to relate to world faiths was a daily concern. Nothing was as simple as the mission agencies based in Europe or the USA anticipated. Immigration brought increasing numbers of members of these faiths to Europe and America, especially from the 1960s onward. The challenge was now in the streets and workplaces of the 'home' churches. Particularly since 9/11 in New York and 7/7 in London, we have been challenged to return to our scriptures—hence these twelve Bible studies, selected from dozens of possible passages.

In 2007, 138 Muslim scholars wrote a famous detailed letter to the Pope and Christian leaders everywhere, quoting the New Testament command to love God and love our neighbour, and calling on Christians and fellow Muslims to live by this command, for we will all be judged by it. Who, then, is God, and who is our neighbour? For Christians, the question means being able to explain who is Christ, and why the cross and resurrection (Colossians 1:15–20). Here is a final challenge to each reader: how can we make this command real locally, as well as globally?

FURTHER READING

Wesley Ariarajah, *The Bible and People of Other Faiths* (WCC, 1985).

Kenneth Cracknell, *In Good and Generous Faith* (Pilgrim Press, 2006).

Israel Selvanayagam, *Relating to People of Other Faiths: Insights from the Bible* (CSS, 2004).

Andrew Wingate, *Celebrating Difference, Staying Faithful* (DLT, 2005).

Church of England Doctrine Commission, *The Mystery of Salvation* (Ch. 7) I (CHP, 1995).

See www.acommonword.com for the letter from 138 Muslim scholars, and dozens of Christian responses.

'Generous Love: the truth of the Gospel and the call to dialogue' (The Anglican Consultative Council, London, 2008), available at: http://nifcon.anglicancommunion.org: an Anglican approach to inter-religious relations.

Genesis 1—11

We really shouldn't be doing this, you know. Imagine an appreciation of Shakespeare's King Lear that covered only Act I, and that will give you some idea of what I mean. Genesis has 50 chapters, and we will be looking only at the first eleven. What's more, Genesis itself is only Book One of a five-part series: its final editors conceived the Pentateuch as a continuous narrative, for which these eleven opening chapters set the scene. The huge interest that these early chapters have for us now should not blind us to the fact that they were vital, but preliminary, for most of their readers throughout most of history. They set the scene for God's interaction with his people, Israel. That's where the focus of attention is designed by its writers to be. Whereas Genesis covers a few thousand years in a broad sweep, the next few books start to go into detail as the real plot begins to unfold.

But if we don't forget that, perhaps it is all right to treat Genesis 1—11 separately. Its grand scene-setting has carried and continues to carry so much theological weight that it would be hard to do it justice if it was treated just as an introduction. Its authors should be allowed some weight, too, however, in guiding us into the meaning and purpose of these chapters.

Like most, though not all, scholars of Genesis, I am assuming that it is the work of a number of consummate theologians. The latest one, chronologically, is called 'P'—the priestly author—and is often thought to be the theologian who gave the book its final shape, incorporating older material and adding some of his own: he was particularly interested in genealogies, for example. The two other theological traditions we find in Genesis are called 'J' and 'E', after their names for God—Yahweh and Elohim. Yahweh is usually translated 'Lord', and 'Elohim', God. Pretty well everything about these three traditions, from their dates to the extent of their contributions, is debated, but for our purposes it is enough to know that the 'book' of Genesis contains traditions of immense antiquity—perhaps as early as the tenth century BC—and is the reflection of generations of believers and theologians. It is also, of course, the work of the Holy Spirit.

When I quote, I will be using the English of the New Revised Standard Version.

1 The purpose of creation

Genesis 1:1—2:3

This beautifully structured, complex description of the creation is theological, through and through. It is stating the nature of the God who is the main character in all that follows. It seems beyond doubt that this is a deliberate theological restatement of what the Ancient Near East took for granted in its creation myths. While it is not clear that Genesis depends on one particular form of that myth, the stories have certain themes in common, which Genesis 1 boldly opposes in the name of the one true God of Israel.

Throughout Genesis 1, the emphasis is on the sheer, effortless will of God, unlike the mythic deities who can create only out of struggle with opposing forces. They may have to slay dragons in order to create the world, but God simply speaks. In other mythologies, divinities of various kinds vie for honour and battle with each other in the formation of matter—like the sun and moon, for example, deserving of worship in most Ancient Near Eastern cultures. Not so in Genesis.

Perhaps most striking of all is the role of the human creation. In parallel mythologies, human beings are created as serfs so that the gods can sit back and enjoy themselves. In Genesis, human beings are made to share with God in ruling and caring for the creation. Whatever that vexed phrase 'in our image' means about the relationship between God and humanity, it cannot be made to mean less than a deep connection between God and humans, freely given by God. It is not earned by us; it is not won by us through battle; it is not natural to us. Here we have the nature of God displayed, utterly unthreatened, utterly generous.

This is a whole new vision of God and of the purpose of creation. Everywhere there is orderly joy and purpose, interdependence and relation. Everything is very good. That is not what our experience always tells us; it is not what other mythologies—religious, personal, social or scientific—say. It was not the experience of the first hearers of this story, defeated by powerful neighbours, decimated and exiled. But Genesis 1 declares it to be the truth: it is very good.

2 Connected relationships

Genesis 2:4–25

Although many of us have woven Genesis 1 and 2 together in our minds into one seamless whole, just as we have with Matthew's and Luke's nativity stories, if we stop and look, we see that these are actually two separate creation accounts, almost certainly from two different sources initially.

This second story isn't really a 'creation' story, since the world has already been made at the start of it. Instead, it concentrates on the creation of human beings, not as the culmination of the process, as in Genesis 1, but deeply connected with all that God has made. 'Adam', the dust-creature, gets life both from God and from what God has already made—the ground. 'Adam' then joins in the life-making process, nurturing and being nurtured by all that God is making.

The verse that introduces this section, verse 4, is interesting. Here it says, 'These are the generations of the heavens and the earth', but the same phrase in 6:9 and 10:1 is translated 'These are the descendants of…'. It does look as though a theological point is being made here. All life is a 'descendant' of the heavens and the earth: we share the earth's family tree. We know that, through evolutionary science, but Genesis also reminds us of the profound relationships that God has built into creation. When he goes on, later, to choose Abraham and his descendants for his own special purposes, it is not to cut this tribe off from their roots but to nourish the common root of all life.

The mud-creature that God makes knows its proper connectedness. It knows God and can speak with him, and it knows the plants and the animals and can tell them the truth about themselves by naming them. Perhaps that is why it cannot really understand the penalty that eating the fruit of the forbidden tree will bring. To eat from that tree will mean to be cut off from God, from life, from the world. How can the earth-creature possibly imagine that, experiencing only the life of God flowing through all things?

God further deepens his clay person's understanding of interdependence as the source of life by separating it into two. Now human beings know with the utmost intimacy the generative, intertwined nature of life.

3 Knowledge of life

The serpent is not the devil, although so much later reflection on this passage has seen it as such. Verse 1 explicitly says that it is just one of the wild creatures that God has made, though a particularly clever one.

Its cleverness, its 'craftiness', is described with a Hebrew word that can be either a good quality or a bad one, depending upon the circumstances. In the book of Proverbs, for example, it is often translated as 'clever' or 'prudent' (see Proverbs 12:16; 13:16); but in other places it is translated as 'cunning', and it suggests a kind of devious intelligence that tries to ignore God (see, for example, Joshua 9:4).

In its context here in Genesis, it is an important word because it sounds very similar to the Hebrew word translated as 'naked'. We have just been told that the woman and the man are serenely 'naked' (2:25). They are equipped with the kind of intelligence that allows them to fit peacefully and unselfconsciously into the world. When they have disobeyed God and eaten the fruit, they become aware of their 'nakedness'. They will now have to live with a dissonance: they are no longer one with the purposeful, interconnected flow of the created world, and they and all living creatures will suffer from this rupture.

Again, the consummate theologian of this narrative is suggesting something. God made the whole world to be interdependent, full of his own life—its own intelligence, though created, still connected with the creative, life-giving intelligence of its maker. But by allowing the crafty serpent to step out of its role and into the human role, human beings have made a break in the circle of life. They now have a kind of 'knowledge' that they cannot handle. It is like God's creative knowledge, but, since they are not God, what they create is not 'very good' but broken.

This whole story, then, becomes a kind of commentary on different kinds of knowledge, the creative and the disruptive. This knowledge is not about facts. Instead, it is about whether we can see how all life flows into and out of the life of God, the unbroken flow of being throughout the universe. In other words, it is about 'the generations of the heaven and the earth'.

4 The first murder

Although Adam and Eve no longer live with God in Eden, they are not otherwise cut off from him. They still understand that creativity flows from God, and that the human ability to reproduce is a powerful symbol that connects us back to our source.

Now, though, the break that was introduced in the previous chapter, in the flow of life from God through his world, is about to become much wider with the murder of Abel. Now the real force of that disruption becomes clear as death enters what was once the shining circle of life.

It is dismayingly unclear why God chooses Abel's offering and not Cain's. Perhaps this ignorance about the divine purpose is, itself, one of the results of the rift between God's knowledge and that of human beings. The echo between God's words to Cain in 4:7 and to Eve in 3:16 does encourage us to make this connection. In the world before Adam and Eve's choice, there was no need to speak of 'mastery': the man and the woman fitted together as partners. Similarly, before Adam and Eve chose to 'know' good and evil, there was no need to exercise 'mastery' over sin. But now Cain knows the struggle to choose to trust God when God's purposes are hidden.

The ground has not chosen to 'know' apart from God, and it cries out with Abel's blood. The ground knows that this life flowed from it and should not now be flowing backwards into it again. Cain has made an enemy of the earth from which he is descended.

Too late, Cain longs to reconnect. He cries out with terror at the loneliness he has brought upon himself, cut off from the soil and from his human family. No wonder he expects to be killed by anyone who meets him, because how will they recognise what he is, as he stands outside the circle of life?

Just as Adam blamed Eve and Eve blamed the serpent and each sinner blames anyone but themselves, so Cain blames God for what he has brought upon himself. Patiently, God explains that Cain cannot force his own choice upon God, and he cannot read God's nature from his own. God is not a killer but the creator and preserver of life, even Cain's.

What does it tell us about ourselves that the phrase 'the mark of Cain' has come to be synonymous with something cursed, when it is actually a symbol of God's compassionate protection?

5 Children of Cain

Genesis 4:17—5:32

Whatever Cain has done, still his story and that of his descendants is part of the narrative. The creativity of God still lives in Cain's children, even though Cain has so wrenched the stream of life from its course. He and his family help to invent the different ways of life known to human beings as city dwellers or as nomadic herders; they invent art and technology; they prove that God was faithful to his promise to Cain, whatever Cain may have feared. Cain thought he was going to be a solitary wanderer, far from all human contact, but instead he is at the centre of a thriving, inventive community. His story is still part of the 'generations of the heavens and the earth'—but perhaps he does not know that any more?

When we return to Adam and Eve, the connection is made explicit again. Seth's children 'invoke the name of the Lord' (4:26), and chapter 5 starts by reminding us of God's original creative act of making human beings in his own likeness, designed for partnership with each other. The connection between God and his creation, and among the created beings themselves, still holds. Adam can pass on his 'likeness' to his children, just as God put his 'likeness' in humankind.

It is intriguing that Cain's family has a long list of inventions to its credit, but Seth's family has only one: prayer. Is it this prayer that enables chapter 5 to start again, with the remembrance that people are made in God's likeness? That likeness was always a gift. It was not a property of the earth from which the human creature was made. So it is something that can be mislaid, and can only be retrieved as a gift, through prayer.

I'm afraid I can't pass on a really convincing explanation of the extraordinary ages ascribed to these patriarchs, because I haven't come across one. In the 17th century, Archbishop Ussher worked out, using these figures, that God must have created the world in 4004BC. He was probably wrong.

6 Anguish and faithfulness

Genesis 6

At last! Daughters! They have been mentioned in passing in some of the genealogies in chapter 5, but now, briefly, they take centre stage, even if the role they play is rather dubious.

It is a matter of considerable debate just who the 'sons of God' are. It would seem strange if they were divine beings of some kind, when Genesis has so far insisted upon God the Creator as the sole divinity in the universe. But it is possible that these 'sons' are created beings who are neither human nor divine, sharing some characteristics with each. For example, like God, they see that the human creation is very good—or 'fair', as verse 2 puts it—but, like humans, they 'take' what they find good, as Eve did in 3:6.

Either way, what God sees is a horrible mess, in which all the beautiful order of creation is ruined. Instead of the steady flow that Genesis 1 describes of one stage of creation into the next, each dependent upon the other, now everything is confused. The ongoing effect of the human attempt to 'know' separately from God's life-giving knowledge is wreaking havoc, so that the divine creativity that human beings used to be able to bring to the world through their likeness to God is now turned to destruction.

Genesis wants us to hear God's anguish, but it also expects us to pick up the hints about God's faithfulness. We know that God is not going to 'blot out' all that he has made, because we have the careful record of the generations of the heavens and the earth from its inception, and we have Noah.

Noah's name means 'relief from work' (5:29) or 'rest', and Noah 'found favour' with God (v. 8). Of course, Genesis does not know of the woman who will find favour with God and carry the seed of the new humanity in the safe ark of her body.

Guidelines

It is usual to think of Genesis 1—3 as 'the creation narrative', but actually the whole of Genesis 1—11 is about the creation. It takes the whole of these eleven chapters to get the world to the point where it is recognisable as the world we live in.

At the point at which we have paused, creation is hanging by a thread, and that thread is Noah. Many things will be different after the flood, but there will also be continuity, thanks to Noah—or perhaps, more truthfully, thanks to God.

So far, these *Guidelines* notes have avoided many controversies that seem to be the obvious ones connected with the creation accounts in Genesis. For example, nothing whatever has been said about 'science and religion' in Genesis 1—3. For many, this is a horribly painful area, where biblical authority seems to be under attack.

But is it possible that we have set the Bible up by ignoring what it tells us itself? Genesis gives us two accounts of the origins of life, one in chapter 1 and one in chapter 2. That is surely a hint that this is a theological discourse, not a scientific treatise. As God reminds Job, we were not there when he made the world, and if we had been, we wouldn't have had a clue what was going on.

That is not to say that none of the Bible is factually true, only that common courtesy to this authoritative text requires us to listen to what it says about itself before demanding that it answer our questions.

The creation stories in Genesis take the assumptions common to their time and critique them in the light of their knowledge of God. Creation is not born out of violence or indifference or power struggle, but out of peaceful, powerful, loving intelligence. That is a critique we can still apply to the creation myths of our own time.

1 Noah's flood

Genesis 7—8 (i)

'Many waters cannot quench love, neither can floods drown it' (Song of Solomon 8:7) could perhaps stand as a summary of the theological heart of the story of Noah's flood.

There are several versions of this story of a great and destructive flood, deriving from Mesopotamia. Both the Gilgamesh epic and the Atrahasis cycle include stories that bear a marked similarity to Noah's flood. (You can read both of these on the web, in a number of different forms.) In each, divine anger causes the flood, with its devastation of life. In each, the obedient man and his boatful are the only survivors. Gilgamesh even has the birds being sent out to prospect for dry land. It is impossible to be sure quite which form of these stories the Genesis theologians knew, but it is clear that, as with the creation stories in chapters 1 and 2, what is going on is a deliberate reinterpretation of common themes.

So, for example, Genesis' received stories speak of conflict between the gods, some of whom want to destroy the world and some of whom don't. The people who survive do so because the main character happens to be in favour with one of the gods, who lets him in on the secret of what is about to happen. The gods who created the flood are taken aback to find that anyone is left alive at the end. They are also frightened of the power of the flood, which is not entirely in their control.

In all of these vital details, Genesis is different. God acts alone and is in complete command of the situation throughout. It is by God's careful provision that examples of all that he has made are to be preserved. The terrifying chaos of the flood is neither terrifying nor chaotic to God. He sets a pattern of days—days before the flood, days during the flood, days as the flood retreats—all symmetrical and orderly, like rows of knitting.

There is no attempt to hide or to explain the destructiveness of God's flood, but equally there is no attempt to hide or to explain God's tenderness to Noah, as he shuts up the doors of the ark, like a mother pulling up the sides of a baby's cot.

2 Restoration

Genesis 7—8 (ii)

God's memory and God's action are not separable. When God 'remembers' his people in Exodus 2:23–25, it is the start of their liberation from Pharaoh. It is as though what God 'remembers' is his own nature and his love for his creation.

So now, at the beginning of chapter 8, God once again restrains the waters, as he did in Genesis 1, to allow the dry land to emerge. Once again, the wind of life blows over the waters. Once again, life comes forth at God's command.

For those of us unduly influenced by the Noah's ark toys we had as children, it is worth rereading 7:2–3. There are certainly matched pairs of animals, but there are also bigger family groups on the ark.

As always, the effortless mastery of the writing in these chapters is breathtaking. We are expected to be highly attentive and intelligent readers. We are expected, for example, to notice that in the story of Noah's flood, time is measured in days again, as it was in the first creation narrative. Creation, devastation and restoration all happen in patterns of weeks and of repeating numbers of days. God's rhythm and order are still implicit, even in the flood.

As God spoke to bring creation into existence, so now God speaks to Noah and brings him out of the ark to resume the life of creation. God's command to the first human creature is repeated to Noah: 'Be fruitful and multiply' (8:17).

The deliberate echoes between creation and restoration after the flood also highlight the differences, however. God no longer sees that it is 'very good'. Instead, he sees that 'the inclination of the human heart is evil' (8:21). But the faithfulness of God is not affected by faithless humanity. God will remember Noah for ever and, in remembering, God will be himself.

3 A covenant with Noah

Genesis 9

Turn back to Genesis 1:28–31 and compare it with Genesis 9:1–7. In each case, God blesses the human beings and describes what their relationship will be with the rest of creation. In each case, human beings are to 'be fruitful and multiply'. But whereas in Genesis 1 their dominion over the earth is to be an image of God's own, and so to be part of the relationship between Creator and creatures, now the rest of creation is afraid of human beings. Instead of being about life-giving orderliness, 'dominion' has now become a concept implying mastery, power and dread. Whereas in Genesis 1 human beings were vegetarians, now they are permitted to eat other living creatures. The balance of creation has changed.

Two things, though, remain fixed. The first is that human beings are not to imagine that they now have God's powers of life and death. Even though they can eat God's animals, the life in those animals belongs to God. God is not careless of life and death, whether of humans or animals. Each death is remembered by God.

The second fixed point is, of course, God himself. God makes a covenant with Noah and with all living creatures, promising that he will always be their faithful God. Whether they remember or not, God will remember. This treaty has no binding clauses for Noah and creation, only for God. God voluntarily curtails his own freedom of action. After this, God will not deal with evil by wiping out everything that it feeds on. This is not to say that God will not deal with evil at all, since God is not short of ideas, but this theology of the faithfulness of God to faithless creation is going to lead directly to the cross.

There is a heaviness about this passage in Genesis, as God accepts the new, marred, diminished state of creation. Even Noah, the blameless man who carried the remnants of creation safely through the flood, forgets God in drink and makes his own family pay for it.

4 The family line of Noah

Genesis 10

These are no longer the generations of the heavens and the earth, but the generations, the family line, of Noah. The innate interconnectedness of all life, with itself and with its Creator, is now masked. People trace their line back with pride, but they do not realise how far they could trace it if only they remembered. They could trace it back to the dust, and know their dependence upon God, and understand that their life is a gift.

We who are reading Genesis as a continuous narrative can see these threads. So when, at the end of chapter 10, we are told that from Noah's sons came all the peoples of the earth, we know that God's commission, 'be fruitful and multiply', is being fulfilled. We also see the slender ribbon of continuity, back to the beginning, forward to the future, coming safely through the waters under God's protection. Can you hear the baptismal echoes there?

People have done a lot of work in tracing these names and their meanings through other records, biblical and non-biblical. For some of the names there are other sources, and for others there are not. But this genealogy is deliberately connecting past and future, deliberately 'remembering', in imitation of God. Many of Israel's territorial neighbours, friends and enemies, are mentioned in this list, reminding the reader of the unity of all human life. This unity is a given in creation, whatever we might do to unmake it.

The children of Shem are mentioned last because they are the most interesting to our author. It is from Shem that Abram comes, eventually.

The New Testament also traces Jesus' ancestry in this line. Luke 3:23–38 lays out a genealogy which is very similar to this one. So Jesus is not just the heir and the fulfilment of the covenants with Abram and Noah, but also the heir and fulfilment of the creation of Adam. The faithful God who pledges himself to his creation is also the redeemer: creation and salvation have the same characteristics.

5 The tower of Babel

Genesis 11:1–9

The tower of Babel is the final straw in these accounts of primeval history. First Adam and Eve chose to believe the serpent rather than God, then the daughters of men intermarried with the sons of God, and now, instead of spreading out over the earth to populate and cultivate it, the people decide they would rather live together in one place. Each of these incidents provokes God's wrath.

It is hard for us to understand why God should be seen to react so violently to what has happened. But while it is important to note that the Genesis theologians are deliberately telling a story, not claiming to report God's actual words, they do emphasise the theological importance of these human transgressions.

The creation story of Genesis 1 describes God bringing life and order into being, making relationships of mutuality and reciprocity among all that he creates, but the human beings keep making choices that reduce harmony to chaos again. They do not understand God's music of creation, and they keep forgetting that it is God's, not theirs. They are not the only ones to suffer. The whole creation, designed as a beautiful interlocking web of life, is wrenched out of shape by snatching human hands.

Babel is almost certainly a sly dig at Israel's mighty neighbour, Babylon, whose temple was said to have its head in the clouds and to reach up to the heavens. But here God has to make a special trip even to see Babel, so tiny is it compared to him. Human pride is put in its place, as the people boast that they will make a name for themselves, while in an instant they find that they cannot understand each other at all. What is the point of boasting if no one can understand you? It is not until Pentecost that human language is reclaimed, and then it is received back as a gift from the Holy Spirit, not as an example of human cleverness.

6 A continuing story

Genesis 11:10–32

After Adam and Eve are evicted from Eden, they and their children still speak with God. After the flood, God comes to Noah and makes a covenant with him. But after Babel, there is no reconciling speech.

This does not mean, however, that there is no hope or that God has lost interest in his creation. For now, with quiet patience, we pick up the genealogy again. When, at last, at the beginning of chapter 12, God speaks to Abram, as he spoke to Adam and to Noah, we know the backstory. Abram is not the beginning of a new story but the inheritor of all that has gone before. He inherits the damaged human nature that Adam and Eve passed on (the Bible is not starry-eyed about its heroes) but he also inherits Adam's relationship with God.

God has not changed. He is still faithfully, persistently relating to all he has made, and working to draw it back into relationship with itself and with him. The role for which human beings were created in this circle of life has not been given to others. Every loyal, obedient human being makes the universe sing its true tune, even if only quietly. So when Abram sets out at God's request, our hearts lift.

It is not until Jesus that we see a human being living and breathing the relationship for which we were all meant. But Jesus is not God finally washing his hands of the rest of humanity; Jesus is God's respectful, unswerving, omnipotent commitment to humanity. Jesus is the image that we were made in, and, wherever the Holy Spirit teaches human beings to say 'Abba, Father' in Jesus' name, there is the beginning of the new creation.

Guidelines

These chapters of Genesis are so well known that we can become careless in our use of them and overlook the profundity of the theology they offer. We come to these stories demanding answers to our questions and are baffled to find that Genesis does not always even recognise them.

For example, the creation accounts do not tell us how evil crept into God's world. They do not account for Adam's 'fall'. They simply describe what we all recognise: the dissonance between our understanding and experience of God and our understanding and experience of the world.

Genesis does, however, have an unsentimental perception that the world is made for complementarity, and that human beings keep trampling over the relationships that would allow all created things to be themselves. It also has an unquestioned certainty that God's relationship to what he has made is not changeable. Nothing we do can force him out of the relationship that he himself instituted towards us: he is the Creator, and he has made the world for a purpose. We can make it almost impossible for ourselves to recognise that, but we cannot make it impossible for God to know it, and what God knows happens.

FURTHER READING

Writing on Genesis is so prolific that it is hard to know where to start. In terms of commentaries, Gordon Wenham's Word Biblical Commentary (Nelson, 1987) and Walter Brueggemann's *Genesis* (John Knox Press, 1982) are both outstandingly helpful. Then there are the theological studies of creation, such as Moltmann's *God in Creation* (SCM, 1985), or Colin Gunton's helpful summary chapter on creation in *The Cambridge Companion to Christian Doctrine* (CUP, 1997).

For those who particularly want to pursue the questions of science and religion, I recommend:

Denis Alexander, *Creation or Evolution: Do We Have to Choose?* (Monarch Books, 2008).

Alister McGrath, *Science and Religion* (Blackwell, 1999).

Keith Ward, *The Big Questions in Science and Religion* (Blackwell, 2008).

Luke 10:17—13:35

This is the fourth contribution in our series on Luke's Gospel, begun for Christmas 2009. It is also the last for the time being. We will return to Luke, to cover the second half of the Gospel, in a few years' time. (In 2011 we will be looking at part of Matthew's Gospel.)

The 'infancy narratives' highlighted three themes—expectations, reversal and the call for obedience—and we have seen these developed in chapters 3—10. Jesus defied expectations. He was profoundly different from contemporary religious figures in his power, his teaching and his manifesto of reversal: the rich being sent empty away, the good news being preached to the poor, welcome and forgiveness to the wicked. Alongside this we have heard the repeated call for response to Jesus' teaching, to Jesus himself and to God.

In the next three weeks we will be challenged to seek first the kingdom of God. We are to seek it wholeheartedly, not being swayed by worry, greed or the opinion of others. We are to seek it urgently: there is a window of opportunity that will close. We are to seek it with simplicity and directness; and, copying Jesus, we are to have compassion on those who are struggling to find it, using our knowledge and experience to their benefit.

Unless otherwise stated, quotations are taken from the NRSV.

4–10 October

1 Revelation

Luke 10:17–24

We concluded our readings in Luke's Gospel three months ago with Jesus sending out the 72 disciples to share in his work of announcing the kingdom. As we pick up the story again, they return to him with joy at what they have experienced. What have the last few months brought for you?

This rich passage can be split into three parts—what it says about God the Father, about Jesus and about us. Regarding God, it makes clear that, whatever appearances might suggest, it is God's will that is sovereign. The disciples should not be caught up in the success of their mission. What matters is that their names are written in heaven, and their names are there because God has written them, not because of what the disciples have done. Similarly, the wise and learned might search for God, but knowledge of God comes only to those whom God chooses.

Regarding Jesus, this passage is explicit about Jesus' unique role. The single word 'Son' is used as a title (v. 22), which seems to be a development from 'Son of God' in the sense that we find it in Luke 1:26–38. Jesus is simply 'the Son' in a pairing with 'the Father', whom he uniquely reveals. Talk of 'uniqueness' can raise anxieties, given our concerns for religious tolerance. Perhaps all that can be said is that this passage does not ascribe a unique role to the church or 'Christian doctrine', but states that all true knowledge of God the Father comes from God and through the 'human face of God', Jesus. Indeed, I would go further and suggest that such revelation from God can come through Jesus without Jesus' role being recognised—just as the revelation of God in the Old Testament was actually through Jesus, even though he was unknown at the time.

Regarding the disciples, the reference to Jesus seeing Satan's fall (v. 18) is intriguing. The 'fall of Satan' often refers to his 'fall from grace'—Satan being an angel of God who disobeyed God (see Ezekiel 28:1–19). This idea is given a different twist in Revelation 12, when Satan is said to be 'thrown down' from heaven as a result of a holy war. Here in Luke it seems that the disciples' activities cause Satan to fall (compare Revelation 12:10–11). There is certainly the sense that, as disciples, we are caught up in something bigger than we might imagine. But there is also the recollection that, in Ezekiel, Satan falls because of his pride. The disciples need to avoid glorying in their newfound power. After all, God chooses the weak—the infants (v. 21).

The final verse, with its talk of seeing and hearing, points back to the verse from Isaiah quoted in relation to the parable of the sower (8:10). Revelation is given to those who respond to Jesus.

2 Who is my neighbour?

Luke 10:25–37

What is at the heart of this well-known story? I believe that the key is in verse 29, the hinge between Jesus' exchange with the expert in the law and the parable: 'wanting to justify himself, he asked… "And who is my neigh-bour?"' The legal expert was not justifying himself in the sense of making himself right with God. Rather, he was justifying his role as a teacher of the law, justifying the particular approach to understanding God's will that was at the heart of much Jewish thinking at the time, and is prevalent today.

Jesus agrees with the man about the summary of the law (v. 27), but seems to think that nothing more is needed: 'Do this, and you will live' (v. 28). Yet this will not do for the lawyer, or for many today. We don't want an open-ended call to love; we want set criteria—things we must do, which, if we tick off, will make us OK. The same logic was behind the effort of religious experts in Jesus' day, who went to great pains to define everything. Their mo-tives may have been good—to ensure they were fulfilling God's commands correctly. Yet, Jesus challenges their approach.

Confronted with a well-intended but false approach to God, Jesus tells a parable (compare Luke 15), and in doing so, he subtly undermines the lawyer's approach. According to the religious lawyers, the priest and the Levite were definitely neighbours to the man ('neighbour' was understood as meaning 'fellow Jew'), yet their concern to avoid ritual impurity (for example, by touching his dead body) meant that they were 'justified' (to use the lawyer's term) in not helping him. On the other hand, they would not have defined a Samaritan as 'neighbour'. However, the answer to Jesus' question, 'Which of these three… was a neighbour to the man?' (v. 36), is obvious. If the lawyer's approach to following God means that the priest and Levite are defined as 'neighbour' but shouldn't actually help, while the Samaritan who is defined as 'not-neighbour' actually acts as a neighbour, it demonstrates the futility of that approach.

The challenge to us is to hold on to the simplicity of the command to love, and to be suspicious of persuasive arguments that end up boxing it in, making it more reasonable, more achievable and more comfortable.

3 Mary and Martha

Luke 10:38–42

This wonderfully evocative story is one of those in the Gospels that we have a tendency to twist, since it doesn't quite say what we want it to. Particularly today, when we are so conscious of different personality types and learning styles, we want it to be a story in which the two sisters' different strengths are appreciated and their complementarity is celebrated. Also, we recognise the claim of unfairness behind Martha's question to Jesus. Why should Martha have to do all the work? We often think of God as a cosmic parent, and we all know that it is important for parents to treat their children equally and fairly.

However, Jesus' response is uncompromising. His words are full of compassion for Martha, yet his answer, 'Mary has chosen better', leaves no room for discussion. Mary's response has been the right one, not Martha's. What is the 'one thing' needed, which Mary has? Presumably, her devotion to Jesus and his teaching. Mary's desire to 'be with Jesus' (as the Twelve were called to be: Mark 3:14) is the correct response. Martha's desire to serve him, to do things for him, in fact leads to worry and distraction. Indeed, there are echoes here of the story of the woman who used much expensive perfume to anoint Jesus' head before the last supper (Mark 14:3–9): the 'uselessness' of her devotion was contrasted favourably with what might have been practically achieved with the money.

There is little more to be said. As we saw from the parable of the good Samaritan, saying more, defining more, can often be a way of escaping from a simple, uncomfortable point. Instead, as both hearers and doers of the word, we are called to examine to what extent we are like Martha, busy in the Lord's service (especially, perhaps, those of us who are formally recognised as ministers) and yet, in the process, distracted from simple devotion to Jesus.

4 The Lord's Prayer

Luke 11:1–4

'Teach us to pray.' 'When you pray, say...' There is a directness and simplicity in the way this prayer is introduced, which matches the directness and simplicity of the prayer itself.

The disciples do not ask for a theology of prayer or pose philosophical questions about how prayer works. They simply want to know how to do it. The same is true in my experience of many today. People inside and outside the church want ideas, suggestions, patterns: they ask, 'What works for you?' or 'How do you do it?' But often we respond with complexities or a reluctance to be open, perhaps nervous about whether we ourselves are doing it 'right'. It's sad that 'how do you do it?' is neither a common topic of discussion within the church nor a topic of relaxed conversation with our friends, neighbours and colleagues, who are often interested to know.

The prayer itself, particularly as presented here in Luke, is extremely brief (it's slightly shorter than Matthew 6:9–13, and much shorter than the version said in church). This in itself should make us think. It begins with the single word 'Father': nothing is dressed up. It expresses a closeness to God, a respectful directness in approaching him, a confidence. There are no long formulae or formalities (not even 'our father', just 'father'). Then come four lines, each as brief and direct as possible—the wish that God's kingdom and holiness may come, and requests for the needs of life, for the restoration of relationships with God and neighbour, and for God's protection.

Why is our prayer not like this? In church we might use the Lord's Prayer, but we add to it many more, lengthier prayers as well. In private, few of us simply pray as set out here. It's not just a matter of style, for when the Lord's Prayer is introduced in Matthew it is preceded by the instruction, 'When you are praying, do not heap up empty phrases as the Gentiles do; for they think that they will be heard because of their many words' (6:7). Surely this challenges the practice of turning the Lord's Prayer into a model, producing prayers that expand on each of its phrases at great length.

This is not easy. Perhaps we can all reflect again on our own prayer in the light of this prayer that Jesus taught us, most of all recognising its confidence, directness and simplicity.

5 Ask for what you need

Luke 11:5–13

When Jesus uses human stories to talk about God, the key step is 'how much more…?' (This was a standard Jewish way of arguing at the time; we see it in Paul—for example, Romans 5:9–10). The friend will get up at midnight and give whatever is needed, even though it is inconvenient. We can get what we need by asking, even when we are asking a friend who does not really want to help. How much more, then, will we get what we need when we ask God, who does want to help? But we do require the courage and confidence to ask. This point continues in the next saying (vv. 9–10), which emphasises that the first move lies with the one praying: they must ask, seek and knock, before the answer can come. We should have confidence that a positive response will come, and this confidence will make it easier to ask, but it is still necessary to ask.

The questions in verses 11–12 develop the point further. One reason for not being bold to ask might be the fear that asking will have a bad result, or that we might ask and then receive the wrong thing. Sadly, we often think of prayer as a type of magic, as if it is powerful but can do us harm if we get it wrong. Jesus' two questions illustrate the foolishness of these concerns. Human fathers do not give their children bad things in response to their requests, so we need not fear that requests to God will produce bad results. God can be trusted. The 'joke' heard often in churches, 'Be careful what you pray for', is woefully unChristian. My children do not need to be careful not to ask their dad for things that will harm them; nor do God's children.

There are two further points. First, the unrestricted nature of Jesus' words, 'everyone who asks receives' (v. 10), have caused much discussion. Is Jesus saying that God will give whatever is prayed for? This question ignores the point of his teaching, which is that prayer should not be seen as a contract or bargain, but as an expression of dependency on a loving Father. A father will not always give a child what is asked for, but nor will a father just ignore his child's request. Second, the mention of the Holy Spirit at the end of verse 13 can seem surprising, since the story leads us to think of more practical needs. Its effect, though, is to highlight that God's Spirit is the greatest of good gifts, which further emphasises that God holds nothing back from those who turn to him as his children.

6 For me or against me?

Luke 11:14–28

This passage, containing a number of different sayings about demons, revolves around the idea that there is a choice to be made: there are, in the end, only two sides. Thus it is aptly concluded with the exchange between Jesus and the woman in the crowd. Even the closest of human bonds are immaterial; what matters is whether we do, or don't, obey the word of God.

We see two attempts to fudge the boundaries. Some people suggest that what looks like God's work (Jesus driving out the demons) is really the work of Satan—or at least might be, hence the need for a sign. Jesus will have none of this, presenting two arguments from experience. First, if Satan fought against himself, his kingdom would have long since collapsed. Thus, the fact that there is still much evil in the world disproves their suggestion. Satan is not like that, which is exactly why it takes a great work of God to break his stranglehold. Second, if they accept that God works through other exorcists, why not through Jesus? This boundary cannot be fudged: it is God at work in Jesus; it is God's kingdom that is breaking in.

Nor can the boundaries be fudged the other way. Those who are not part of Jesus' movement are not helping (v. 23). The logic of this verse is probably to be found in the following saying about the spirit. The evil spirit leaving the man seems like a good thing, and yet in the end he returns and the man is in a worse state. (Note that Jesus talks of the evil spirit leaving, rather than being driven out of the man.) So it is with those who seem to be doing some good but are not part of Jesus' movement. People are either supporting the incoming 'kingdom of God' or they are hindering it.

Verse 23 seems to contradict Luke 9:50 ('Whoever is not against you is for you'). But in Luke 9, the disciples complain about a man who drives out demons in Jesus' name, but does not 'follow with us'. This is all about the disciples, and Jesus rejects their claim that his work cannot go forward apart from them. Our passage is about Jesus, where there can be no fudge. God's work can go forward outside the church, but not apart from Jesus.

These claims make difficult reading, for often, surely, it is right to make common cause with people who do not share our allegiance to Jesus? This is why the comparison with 9:50 is important. There is nothing here promoting exclusivity in our dealings with others, merely the warning that we ourselves need to be clear about whether we are seeking to obey the word of God and to further the coming of his kingdom.

Guidelines

In different ways, this week's readings have advocated simplicity:

- The simplicity of the command to love our neighbours, uncomplicated by further analysis and definition.

- The simplicity of devotion to Jesus; in the end, it is devotion, not work, that matters, and devotion can't be fudged.
- The simplicity of prayer to a loving Father.

Of course, life is complicated. And yet, if we are to take these passages seriously, we must take a step back and ask whether life—especially with regard to our relationships, motivations and spirituality—should be as complicated as we sometimes make it.

Bring each of these three points in turn before God. Where do you make things unnecessarily complicated?

1 Discern the truth

Luke 11:29–36

This passage divides into two: verses 29–32 on Jonah, and verses 33–36 on darkness and light. Together, they demand that people discern the truth.

The thrust of the saying about Jonah is that people are wrong to ask for a sign (v. 29 perhaps looks back to v. 16), because they have already seen ample evidence that God is with Jesus (compare 10:13–15). The 'Queen of the South' (the 'Queen of Sheba', 1 Kings 10) recognised that God was with Solomon and travelled to listen to him on the basis of far less evidence. Similarly, the people of the wicked city of Nineveh (Jonah 1:2) recognised that God was speaking through Jonah, though he performed no miracles at all. The request for a sign simply demonstrates the people's inability to discern the truth when it is in front of their eyes. Notice also the focus on people—Solomon, Jonah, and Jesus, the one greater than both. Once again we are challenged to see that the message, the sign (v. 30), is Jesus himself. As before, the one thing that cannot be fudged is the way we respond to him.

The sayings about light and darkness are best understood as three inter-connected steps. First (v. 33), the light of God is not hidden but is there for all to see. The second step (v. 34) becomes clearer if we replace 'eye' with 'the ability to see' or 'the ability to discern the truth', and 'body' with 'life'. Whether our life is full of light or not depends fundamentally on our ability to discern the truth, just as whether we are in darkness or light depends fundamentally on the healthiness of our eyes. Step three (v. 35) challenges us to consider whether something that should be giving us light is actually giving us darkness—whether our ability to discern the truth is flawed. Verse 36 then points us back to verse 33, where the lamp is divine revelation, and makes the final connection: our ability to discern the truth is the same as our ability to receive divine revelation. This is certainly possible (our whole body can be full of light) but it is not automatic. Thus, together, these passages assert that the people around Jesus had all the evidence they needed. What mattered was whether or not they discerned the truth: without it, they were in darkness. Indeed, the passage that follows laments the Pharisees' inability to 'see'.

It's challenging to see how to apply this passage to ourselves, who have not encountered Jesus in his earthly ministry. Do *we* have the right to ask for more evidence? The logic, particularly from the comparison with the Queen of the South and Jonah, suggests not. God is apparent in our world, if we have a mind to discern him. 'Ever since the creation of the world [God's] eternal power and divine nature, invisible though they are, have been understood and seen through the things he has made' (Romans 1:20).

2 Woe to the Pharisees!

Luke 11:37–54

This blistering attack on the Pharisees and experts in the Jewish law reveals the heart of Jesus' criticism of them. It marks the opening up of a sharp division between them and Jesus (vv. 53–54), and raises questions that we might do well to ask of ourselves today.

The attack has four parts. First (vv. 39–42), Jesus criticises the Pharisees for a wrong balance and focus in their approach to the law. Yes, God did make the outside of the cup. Yes, the law does contain some purity regulations. Yes, you should tithe the herbs. But what really matters is greed and wickedness, love and justice, and care for the poor.

The second part (vv. 43–44) may bring together two unrelated sayings. They certainly appear separated in Matthew (compare v. 43 with Matthew 23:5–12, and v. 44 with 23:27). They are connected, though, by the idea of being seen. Perhaps the criticism in verse 43 is of an all-too-human desire to demonstrate status. In addition, though, the Pharisees were a reform party within Judaism, seeking to be a light to others, to help others reach God by showing a good example. Jesus claims that rather than being a light to be seen, they are a hidden corrupt darkness (graves caused uncleanness, so an unmarked grave was extremely unwelcome). They do not inspire others by being seen; they corrupt others by what is not seen in them.

The third part of the attack (vv. 47–51) is not so clear. Jesus may be commenting on the literal building of tombs for the prophets. His real point, though, is that the experts 'entomb' the prophets, weighing them down with so much interpretation and regulation that the prophets' message is buried, honouring them in appearances while not following their teaching. (Certainly, Amos and Hosea urged that justice was more important than religious rituals.) Thus they are completing the work of those who killed the prophets.

The fourth part (v. 52, compare v. 46) functions as a summary of the whole. The Pharisees set themselves up as guides for others, to show them what God wanted, but in fact they were hindering the people who listened to them. Whatever the Pharisees' and legal experts' intention, they were, in fact, leading people astray. If they are the eyes of the whole nation, the eyes are bad (11:34–36). As always, when Jesus criticises the religious leadership in his day, the challenge for us is to discern whether Jesus could level the same criticisms at us today.

3 Judgment—by whom?

Luke 12:1–12

This passage continues the criticism of the Pharisees, first using the image of yeast. Yeast is a natural symbol for something that has an impact out of all proportion to its size, but also, within Jewish thought, it always implies a negative impact (see 1 Corinthians 5:8). The Pharisees were a small group in terms of numbers, but their intention was to influence the whole of society. Jesus agrees that they have an impact, but sees it as darkness, not light.

Jesus' point is then developed in a new direction. The Pharisees' system is, in effect, based on worrying about how people will judge us, but the true judge is God. This gives more depth to the charge of hypocrisy. Jesus' point is not that some Pharisees were hypocritical (aren't we all sometimes?) but that their whole approach was hypocritical. In their eagerness to intensify law-observance, they focused on getting the detail of visible observance of the law correct, rather than the more central principles (mercy and justice), which are inherently less visible. But it is those moral aspects that matter most to the God who will judge the heart, and from whom nothing is hidden.

The idea of judgment is then developed. We should fear God rather than fearing humans (as it is claimed the Pharisees do), because he makes the final judgment with eternal consequences (vv. 4–5, 8). This notion of being frightened of God's judgment is rare in the Gospels, and is immediately softened here by the assertion of God's care (vv. 6–7), protection and presence (vv. 11–12). The point is not to motivate through fear of God's judgment, but to point out the stupidity of being concerned more about what people think of us (the visible) than what God does (the hidden).

Verses 8–9 seem to undermine this point, because here what is done before humans does matter. However, the logic is that fear of what people will think pressurises us not to acknowledge Jesus. Again, here is a deep criticism of the Pharisees' system. In some part, it was based on using shame—public criticism—to motivate people to follow God's law. Jesus seems to reject this approach: focusing on human opinion will not produce good effects.

The saying on blasphemy against the Holy Spirit (v. 10), in this context, softens the saying about acknowledging Jesus: although our response to Jesus is crucial, even here mistakes can be forgiven. Of course, we then want to know what 'blasphemy against the Holy Spirit' is. This passage does not make it clear, but a similar saying appears in Mark 3:29, where the context suggests that it means confusing God's work with the work of the devil. If so, the overall point is that we need not fear judgment—even insulting Jesus can be forgiven—as long as we can recognise God at work. (If we can't, we won't be able to turn to God to ask for forgiveness in the first place.)

4 Beware of greed

Luke 12:13–21

Since 11:37, our passages have focused on Jesus' engagement with the Pharisees. We now move on, though this passage is linked to the previous one by the command to 'watch out!' (see 12:1, 15). It is also linked to the next passage by the idea of the foolishness of worrying about material possessions.

It is not clear why Jesus interprets the man's question to him as a display of greed. Perhaps he simply feels used. We should probably not engage in such speculation, and should focus on the teaching that emerges from the incident. The point of the parable is clear: greed is foolish. If the point of the previous passage was 'being concerned about human opinion is foolish', here we have 'being concerned about building up human possessions, or even human security, is equally foolish'. It is important to see that Jesus' criticism is not of the man's wealth but of his attitude to it, his heart and his motivation. His wealth—his highly productive land—has become a trap for him, for his land produces a crop which, rather than being a cause of rejoicing, creates the problem of how to ensure that he loses none of it.

It is easy to let this parable pass over us because we do not consider ourselves wealthy and we do not engage in such obvious greed as the tearing down of barns to build bigger ones. The final verse broadens the teaching, though. It is not just about great riches; it is about the attitude of 'storing up for ourselves'—in effect, focusing on looking after ourselves rather than trusting in God.

It's very easy to be caught up in the belief that we just need to carry on pursuing various goals—the next promotion, the deposit on the house, the partnership in the company, getting the children through school—and then we will turn our focus to God. Effectively, we are saying, 'God, I just need to carry on focusing on worldly things for now. Then, when I have what I need, I will focus on you.' The foolishness is twofold. First, as with the man in the parable, 'for now' will actually continue for ever: there is always the next goal; 'need' is never satisfied. Second, as our next passage will develop, the pursuit of security in our possessions or achievements actually results in worry and anxiety. It does not deliver what it promises.

5 Where is your treasure?

Luke 12:22–34

Jesus' advice that we should not worry is based on two principles. First, there is no need, for God will take care of us. The birds and flowers do not worry and yet he provides for them. Flowers are intricate and amazingly coloured, despite the fact that their life is so short and their beauty achieves nothing. Clearly we are more important than the birds and the flowers. Why worry if there is no need? Second, there is no point in worrying, since we cannot change what is important. We cannot add an hour to our life (just as the man in the previous parable died before he could enjoy all his riches). Why worry if it does not achieve anything? Worry is fundamentally a lack of trust in God, on whom we are dependent. Verses 30–31 provide an apt summary. We should focus our attention and energy on the kingdom of God. Meanwhile, God (called 'Father' to emphasise his compassion and love) will ensure that our needs are met. The existence of needs is not disputed; the point is about what we 'strive for'.

The final three verses (vv. 32–34)—the climax of the teaching on possessions and worry—contain reassurance, advice and warning. The reassurance is that God, their Father, loves the disciples and will give them all they need. They may appear to be insignificant and defenceless (a 'little flock'), but they should not be deceived by appearances: God has chosen to 'give them the kingdom' (as in 6:20). If God has chosen to give them the most important thing possible, they can be reassured that he will provide them with everything else that they need. The advice is that they should 'exchange' their possessions for treasure in heaven, principally by giving to the poor. The reason for this is that treasure in heaven is permanent and secure (remember the man who died after having built his bigger barn, 12:13–21).

Finally, the warning comes, summing up the whole of the chapter since 12:13. The fact is, says Jesus, that your attention and energies (your 'heart') will be focused on the place where you are storing up your treasure. If you are storing up treasure in the form of wealth, it will corrupt you; whatever your intentions, it will gradually absorb your attention and energy. This is why Jesus said, 'Beware of greed!' (12:15): it can creep up and trap you.

6 Be ready

Luke 12:35–48

The second illustration (the thief, v. 39) is the most straightforward and expresses Jesus' basic point. The only way of dealing with a thief is to be constantly prepared. The first illustration makes the same general point: the servants need to be ready for the master's return, whenever that may be. However, it also contains the surprising idea of the master waiting on the servants. The master's return will be good for them in a surprising way.

But who or what are people meant to be ready for? In Jewish thought, it is natural to assume that a story involving a master and servants illustrates the relationship between God and his people. Thus, these stories would be about the need for the Jewish people to be prepared for the moment of God's return to them.

Verse 40 takes the idea further, with its mention of the Son of Man, for Jesus uses this phrase to refer to himself. Also later, in 22:27, he says that he has come to serve others who are sitting at the table, which ties in with the unusual element of the master/servant illustration, and suggests that he is the master in the illustration. It is natural for us to take this as referring to Jesus' second coming, ushering in the fullness of God's kingdom. However, on Jesus' lips, presumably the focus was on God coming to his people in Jesus' earthly ministry. We will see this focus in 19:41–44, when Jesus weeps because the people did not recognise that God was coming to them, in him.

Verses 41–48 ask a further question: 'Who are the servants?' The people in general, or those who devote themselves to God's service (the disciples)? In response, Jesus tells a variation on the first story, introducing a new character—the chief servant or manager. Thus Jesus implies that the servants in the stories stand for the people in general, while the chief servant represents Peter and the disciples. The main point is still the same—be prepared for the master's return—but there is a special message for the chief servant. He has a favoured place, being responsible for the other servants, but he faces the temptation of abusing his power over them (v. 45), with the threat of a terrible judgment as well as the possibility of even greater reward (vv. 44, 46).

Jesus often criticises the Pharisees on the same grounds: they had a favoured place, but misused it (see 11:37–54). The same possibility, leading to the same potential criticism, faced his disciples and faces us today.

Guidelines

This week, our readings have explored how we relate to God and the world around us, and how these two relationships connect. Two challenges emerge:

- To focus on God, not to be swayed by the opinion of others, and not to be distracted by worry or greed.
- To benefit others, to ensure that our impact on those around us is beneficial for them, serving and inspiring rather than abusing or corrupting.

These could be united under the label 'seeking first the kingdom of God', for the kingdom is God-focused but is also good news for others. Is God laying one of these challenges on your heart?

1 Seize the moment

Luke 12:49–59

You can hear the exasperation: 'Do you think that I have come to bring peace?' (v. 51); 'Why do you not know how to interpret the present time?' (v. 56). This sense of eschatology—that time, the present time, is important—is a crucial thread throughout the Gospel (see, for example, the use of 'today' in 4:21; 19:9; 23:43). Luke 1—2 established that something was about to happen: a decisive moment was about to come. Yet the people don't seem to be able to realise it. They might be listening to Jesus but they are failing to respond (10:13–15; 11:29–32). In the language of the previous parable, the master is about to knock on the door, the thief is climbing in through the window, but they have not noticed.

The saying on peace is perhaps surprising. However, Simeon said at the start of the Gospel that Jesus would be 'for the falling and the rising of many in Israel… a sign that will be opposed' (2:34). We have seen this opposition in the increasingly bitter interaction with the Pharisees. Similarly, the saying on acknowledging the Son of Man (12:9–10) implied that the world will be split into two—those who acknowledge Jesus and those who do not. Hence he brings division. In my mind I see a crowded railway platform. Someone is shouting at the people on the platform, telling them the train is about to leave, but most ignore him. In the end, the train will go, and some will be on it and some will be left behind.

In Nazareth, Jesus announced 'the year of the Lord's favour' (4:19).

There is a sense here that 'the year' is running out. Judgment is coming. Therefore the crowds would be wise to learn from a human example (vv. 57–59). They should take this last opportunity to settle things with God, but they seem incapable of realising what is happening around them, that judgment is just around the corner.

Today, most of us are wary of urging people to 'act now' and certainly of suggesting that action is needed because 'judgment is coming'. However, we should recognise that urgency was a key element of Jesus' mission. What might that mean for us? Perhaps a way through is provided by the story of Zacchaeus (19:1–10), where we see urgency for the person (Jesus was passing through Jericho that day; this was Zacchaeus' opportunity, which would not easily come again) without the suggestion that 'the end is nigh'.

2 Time is running out

Luke 13:1–9

Jesus gives a final warning (vv. 1–5), pointing to two disasters that had happened recently. One was 'man-made'—the horrific killing of some Galileans by Roman governor Pilate—and the other 'natural', the collapse of a tower in Jerusalem. Both of these are examples of what everyone is facing. They should not comfort themselves by saying that the people who died were particularly evil and therefore deserved it. This is what the future holds for everyone unless they spot the signs and make peace with God (as the last passage had it). This is perhaps as close as we get to 'fire and brimstone' preaching on Jesus' lips. In the previous passage, we could sense Jesus' exasperation with the crowds; later he will weep for them (19:41–44). Thus we see that 'unless you repent, you will all perish' should be heard as a declaration of frustrated, passionate concern: there is certainly no pleasure in the announcement of coming judgment.

The parable is particularly forceful. The man rightly wants to cut down the tree that is not producing any fruit and is taking up valuable space and attention in his vineyard. What is the point of leaving it there? However, he is persuaded to give it a stay of execution. He will give it one last chance, but that is what it is. People might look at the tree and think, 'It hasn't been cut down—it never will be', but they would be mistaken. God is giving them one last chance to 'produce fruit' (compare 3:8–9; 6:43–45). However, if they do not take it, they will be destroyed (the 'year of the Lord's favour', 4:19, will not last for ever).

Again, many of us find this sense of urgency disturbing, fearing, perhaps, a form of abuse in which people are railroaded into making decisions (something that Jesus would not agree with: see, for example, 14:28–32). Nevertheless, we have to face the fact that urgency is precisely the point here.

3 Healing on the sabbath

Luke 13:10–17

There is a clear break in content between this passage and the previous one. Here we revert to an earlier theme—the clash between Jesus and the religious leaders of his day over what should be done on the sabbath (6:1–11). In this passage, Jesus is on the people's side against the religious leaders (v. 17), while in the previous one he was challenging the crowd itself.

The incident is straightforward: Jesus heals a crippled woman on the sabbath. The question is whether or not his actions were appropriate. The law says that people should not work on the sabbath, which was interpreted by many in Jesus' day as meaning that healing should not be done unless it was urgent. The woman had been crippled for 18 years, so it was clear that, from a medical point of view, the situation was not urgent: it would have kept to the next day. This was clearly the view of the synagogue ruler. Healing is fine, but the sabbath takes priority. Jesus, however, calls him a hypocrite, linking his attitude to that of the Pharisees. The ruler's attitude is hypocritical because it puts the outward form—the keeping of particular regulations—above the inner principles that really matter. Jesus then illustrates what the inner principles of the law really are.

The law allows an animal to be untied and led out to water on the sabbath, despite the fact that this is work, because the animal's welfare is more important than the sabbath. If the welfare of an animal is more important, how much more the welfare of the woman, who in her own way had been 'tied up'? Healing is clearly more important than the sabbath. The sabbath should be a blessing for the people—a time for release. Yet it has been turned into a burden (compare 11:46, where the legal experts are told that they load the people down with burdens while doing nothing to help). There is perhaps a link here to the previous material on urgency. It is all very well to say that, from a medical point of view, the woman's case was not urgent. However, this particular sabbath was her window of opportunity, while Jesus was there; it was urgent, for the moment would pass.

As always, we should reflect on whether our own religious practices and culture have parallels with the Pharisees'. When do we, in practice if not intentionally, put outward forms and particular ways of doing things above the underlying principles and the command to love our neighbour?

4 From small beginnings

Luke 13:18–21

These two simple illustrations have the same basic point. The kingdom of God looks small and insignificant but it will grow to have an enormous effect. The first illustration focuses on the kingdom's growth—far beyond what initial impressions might have suggested. The birds demonstrate how substantial the plant has become, but they also suggest that the kingdom will be something attractive and beneficial to others. The second illustration focuses more on the effects of the kingdom: the yeast transforms a huge amount of flour. We can note in passing how these two illustrations form a gender-pair (others in Luke include 15:3–7 and 8–10), drawing on the life experience of normal men and women to communicate the message.

Why are these verses included at this point in the Gospel? Perhaps as an encouragement. Chapters 11—12 have been quite gloomy, full of opposition to Jesus and his growing exasperation with the lack of response among the people and the religious leadership. Success seems to be very limited. Then, in the previous passage, we have had the healing of just one woman. Is this what the kingdom will amount to? (Indeed, the following passage asks whether Jesus' announcement of the kingdom will only affect a small number.) No, but this one healing is a mustard seed; the rescue of one woman is a small beginning from which the kingdom will grow. These illustrations encourage us that from small beginnings something great can grow.

This is certainly an encouragement that many of us today need to hear. Our society celebrates outward, immediate success. We want to see and measure results quickly. This attitude is ill-suited to the work of the kingdom, which often develops slowly and organically, whether in individuals or communities. It is interesting to hold this point alongside the urgency that was stressed in 12:35—13:9. There certainly seems to be a tension between urgency and a recognition of the slow, unforced growth of something small. Perhaps there is a paradox here. Perhaps it is resolved to some extent by noticing that the urgency is a challenge to individuals to respond, to recognise the signs of the times and seize the opportunities in front of them, while this parable speaks more to those outside the process looking on—to the church and those committed to proclaiming the kingdom of God. They, and we, need to be encouraged that even if, to us, things look faltering and small, they may still be destined to have a great impact in the end.

5 Second-hand won't work

Luke 13:22–30

Jesus is asked an obvious question: are many people going to be saved (or enter the kingdom)? Is it something only for the religious elite, or for the normal people? Jesus, however, makes a different point in his reply, echoing his earlier teaching on being prepared and seeing the signs (12:35—13:9). Speculating on how many will be saved is not productive. What the questioner should do is to make every effort to get into the kingdom. (Note that, by referring to the 'narrow door', Jesus does seem to suggest that only a few will be saved, or at least that it is not easy.) There is also an urgency here. Soon the house owner will close the door and it will be too late. Thus, Jesus refuses to be drawn into a theological argument but instead focuses on calling the individual in question to make a response. This fits with the general tone of so much of his interaction with the religious leaders of his day: they want to talk and debate, while he wants response and action.

Jesus does not stop here. The people in the illustration claim to have a special relationship with the master. However, it is a second-hand relationship. They do not actually know him; they have just been in the same place at the same time. This is not sufficient, and the master denounces them as unknown to him. The mention of the 'streets' points back to 10:13–15, where Jesus denounced various Galilean towns in which he had spent much time, because they had still not repented. Indeed, Jesus claims, even the great wicked non-Jewish cities of history would have repented had they had the same chance (see also 7:31–35; 11:29–32). Jesus is not rejecting the idea that there is a special relationship between God and the Jewish people—the great Jewish heroes of the past will enter the kingdom of God (v. 28)—but such a relationship needs to be first-hand. Relying on our proximity to those who are close to God, or a family or racial link with them, will not work. Jesus' listeners can't simply rely on the fact that they are Jewish. There is a reversal coming. It is not a complete reversal: it is not that all who were first will be last. Abraham and many of his descendants will be at the feast in the kingdom of God. But some who were last (non-Jews) will be first, and some who were first (Jews) will be last. The point for the questioner and the crowd is clear. Relying on their Jewishness, and the fact that Jesus came to them, is futile. What matters is whether Jesus knows them. For that, they must make an effort: they must respond to him.

6 Weeping for Jerusalem

Luke 13:31–35

Herod had earlier imprisoned and killed John (3:19–20; 9:9). Jesus, in many respects, was continuing down a similar path to John, so it is not surprising that Herod was also seeking to eliminate him. More surprising, perhaps, is that some Pharisees warned Jesus of this desire. However, although Jesus attacks the Pharisees on various occasions, it would be mistaken to assume that no Pharisees admired what he did: indeed, he was often invited to dine with them (for example, 11:37; 14:1). Jesus' reply is that neither Herod nor anybody else can prevent God's will from coming about. His course is set for him—to die in Jerusalem (9:22, 44), as did the prophets before him—and he will not be diverted from it.

The mention of Jerusalem causes Jesus to remember the city with sadness. Even though it has rejected the messengers sent to it (see 11:47–51; 20:9–16), Jesus still has great compassion on its inhabitants. The stumbling block is that they have not been willing: they have refused to respond. This is truly a tragedy, which will result (or perhaps already has resulted) in their being abandoned by God. Their 'house' (normal language for the temple) is desolate: God has deserted it. Later (19:38), when Jesus enters Jerusalem, his disciples cry out, 'Blessed is the king who comes in the name of the Lord' (quoting Psalm 118:26), but there is no positive response from the city, and Jesus immediately weeps over it because it did not 'recognise the time' of God's coming (19:44). Jerusalem did not respond when it had the chance; in this it is no different from the towns and villages of Galilee (10:13–15). It will now not see him again until the moment when all is revealed, and it is too late—and the door to the house is closed (13:25).

We should recognise the passion and anguish in Jesus' words. The people of Jerusalem do have a special place in God's heart, which makes their lack of response all the more heartbreaking. We should also understand this manner of speaking—personifying whole cities and regions—for the rest of Luke and its sequel Acts demonstrate that many individuals in Jerusalem did respond to Jesus and became his followers (see Acts 6:7). Nevertheless, 'the city' did not. Jesus' passion and anguish, born out of his love and care for people, are salutary for us all. Do we care enough to be caught up in the same emotion?

Guidelines

Many of us are rightly hesitant about urgency in religion. It smacks of pressurising people, with a timetable of our making, not of theirs. Certainly there is no justification for letting our timetable affect others, but we must recognise that God may have his own timetable and, more generally, that life does not carry on the same for ever. Moments of opportunity come and they go.

Our passages this week have illustrated both sides of the work of proclaiming the kingdom. Jesus' message is one of urgency. People need to stop discussing and pondering, and respond decisively while they have the chance. We have also seen the other side: Jesus does not treat others as 'problems to be solved'. They are not just numbers in his plan; urgency does not justify a utilitarian approach on his part. He is genuinely grief-stricken at their lack of response; he spends time focusing on the plight of a single woman; he teaches that small beginnings are important and worthwhile.

It's difficult to hold these two emphases together. Often, those who grasp the urgency seem to have little compassion for individuals. Others, with a great belief in the quiet work of God in individuals, shun any idea of urgency. What is your natural tendency? What might God be saying to you?

Psalms 14 (13) to 25 (24)

In these two weeks, reflection is centred on a second group of twelve psalms. The Psalter is the prayer book of Israel (though we do not know precisely how the psalms were preserved and handed down), so in reflecting on the Psalms we enter into the prayer life of the people of God as they were guided towards and prepared for the coming of the Messiah. The Psalms must also form the background of the prayer life of the holy family and of Jesus himself. Quotations from and allusions to the Psalms in the Gospels throughout Jesus' ministry show how much they must have featured in his thoughts. The Psalter is the book of the Old Testament quoted most frequently in the New.

The original language of the Psalms is Hebrew. Now Hebrew is a craggy and succinct language. Especially in poetry, each word is pregnant with sense and allusion. The eight Hebrew words of Psalm 19:7 are rendered by 28 in English. This can give the impression of a series of uncoordinated hammer blows of sense or imagery. The ancient Greek version of the Psalms (in the Septuagint, so called because, according to legend, it was produced by 70 translators) often differs widely from the Hebrew text that we now have, and may represent a Hebrew version earlier than and different from what we now possess. Consequently, English versions of the Psalms often differ considerably as the translator struggles to express the sense and implications of the words. The translator must also make decisions about whether to reproduce the 'cragginess' of the poetry (similar to the English poetry of G.M. Hopkins and T.S. Eliot) or whether to offer a smoother and more flowing English text.

This group consists mostly of short psalms, though it also includes the third-longest of the whole Psalter. Most of them are in the Wisdom tradition, reflecting on the values and qualities of the life given us by the Lord. One particular image that recurs frequently in them is God as Rock, our source of stability and refuge in need.

These notes are based on the Revised Grail Psalter and, unless otherwise stated, on the New Jerusalem Bible.

A note on numbering: The Revised Grail Psalter, in accordance with the Roman Catholic tradition, uses the numbering of the Greek version of the Psalms, rather than the Hebrew. In the Greek text, the Hebrew Psalms 9 and 10 are shown as a single psalm—Psalm 9. Thus the Greek version stays one number behind until Psalm 148. Because many Protestant versions adopt the Hebrew numbering (following Luther's preference), however, both numbers have been given in psalm references between 10 and 147. You will find the Hebrew number given first, with the Greek in brackets afterwards.

1 The fool has said in his heart

Psalm 14 (13)

This is a Wisdom psalm, teaching about folly and wisdom. It is built on a contrast, with the turning point in the middle of verse 4; the first half describes the wicked, the second half those whom the Lord will save.

The fool in the first half, who says in his heart, 'There is no God', is not a deep-thinking atheist announcing a carefully considered opinion. There are many sorts of fool, and the word used here for 'fool' (nabal) is more of a coarse lout, who understands nothing and is rough and insensitive. The perfect example of this sort of person is Nabal, the rich and loutish landowner in 1 Samuel 25, who refuses to pay David for guarding his crops ('Nabal is his name and nabal his nature,' says his wife, as she prepares to snuggle into David's bed). So the first part of the psalm characterises the insensitive lout, whose loutishness expresses itself in a practical inability to appreciate divine values. The psalm stresses how widespread such fools are, with the triple 'No one who does any good… not one… not one'.

For Christians, this denunciation has an especial force because it is quoted by Paul in Romans 3, when he is summing up the depravity of all humanity—first Gentiles, then Jews—with a string of scriptural quotations. After outlining the failure of Gentiles to obey natural law and the failure of Jews to obey the Law of Moses, Paul emphasises that this is not surprising by giving six scriptural quotations about the utter depravity of the human race. This is the depravity from which we are saved by Christ's obedient self-sacrifice: 'just as one man's trespass led to condemnation for all, so one man's act of righteousness leads to justification and life for all' (Romans 5:18, NRSV).

The second half of the psalm, however, gives the three groups of people whom the Lord will protect and rescue. First (v. 5), there is 'the righteous generation' or, in less formal language, those who live according to God's Law, appreciating and endeavouring to live within its promises. Righteousness, of course, consists not in earning salvation—no one can do that—but in reliance on God's promises. Second (v. 6), there are the poor—those who, having no resources of their own, turn to God for help. Third (v. 7), all Israel will draw salvation from Zion.

2 Lord, who may abide in your tent?

Psalm 15 (14)

This psalm is a little litany of requirements for keeping company with God. Some commentators have interpreted it rather woodenly as a sort of interrogation to be conducted at the door of the sanctuary. It is more a reflection on the moral qualities required, somewhat similar to Psalm 1. To describe the list as a set of ten commandments goes, perhaps, a little too far. The qualities are expressed first positively, in terms of what we should do (vv. 2, 4), and then negatively—what we should not do (vv. 3, 5). The first set of qualities concerns telling the truth; the second centres on business dealings. Both sets are as relevant to today's world as to the world of the original psalmist. So often, public morality seems to approve anything you can get away with. If you can win your case by concealing or twisting evidence, that is considered fair play. If fraudulent financial dealings are well enough disguised, that is considered fair game. The morality outlined by the psalmist goes much further.

It is, however, the first line that I find arresting, with the words 'abide in your tent'. The psalmist is phrasing closeness to God in terms of the tent of meeting. During the desert wanderings, the tent of meeting was the mobile sanctuary where God would reveal himself, where the Lord would 'talk to Moses face to face, as a man talks to his friend' (Exodus 33:11). Israel always yearned for the simplicity of the desert relationship with the Lord, which they saw as the honeymoon period when Israel was faithful to the Lord. There is a richness about desert spirituality that cannot be rivalled. When you are alone in the desert, you have no artificial support or distraction. It can be both daunting and inspiring. It certainly leads to focus and self-knowledge, and to that wonderful relationship, 'fear of the Lord'.

The verb used in the Hebrew for 'abide' or 'dwell' is the word from which the shekinah of the Lord is derived, a word full of dread and mystery—that awesome glory of the Lord that no human being can look upon. It is the word to which the prologue of John's Gospel refers: 'the Word was made flesh and dwelt among us'. The whole psalm is about dwelling with the Lord, and cannot but call to mind the words of Jesus: 'Those who abide in me and I in them bear much fruit' (John 15:5, NRSV).

3 O Lord, it is you who are my portion and cup

Psalm 16 (15)

To avoid the accusation of neglecting problems, a preliminary word must be said about verses 3–4: they are very obscure, and the text differs in Greek and Hebrew. The mention of 'holy ones in the land' and 'other gods' may imply that the author once revered some earth deities or agricultural spirits, from whom he has now turned to worship the Lord with all his heart.

The main theme, however, is delight in the Lord, perhaps by contrast to the earth deities. The phrase 'you who are my portion and cup' (v. 5) expresses the firm and lasting link between God and the psalmist. In the Christian further understanding of the psalm, it is even often understood as an allusion to the sacramental, eucharistic cup that mediates the presence of Christ—a legitimate application, though it was certainly not part of the original sense of the psalm.

Furthermore, in Peter's speech at Pentecost, a full quotation of verses 8–11 is used to prove the resurrection of Christ: 'You will not... allow your holy one to see corruption' (Acts 2:27). In accordance with the Christian way of seeing Christ everywhere in the Old Testament, 'your holy one' is understood as a reference to Christ, and these verses are seen as a direct prediction of the resurrection.

Even without such a literal understanding, this is one of the passages in the Psalms that express the longing for eternal company with the Lord, and a belief that God will not abandon for ever those who commit themselves to him. The psalmist cannot rest satisfied with the powerless half-life of

Sheol, where it is impossible even to praise God. Exactly what the psalm-ist hopes is not yet clear. Does 'my body shall rest in safety' (v. 9) imply a hope in bodily resurrection? This hope becomes explicit only in the book of Daniel, less than two centuries before Christ. As with similar mentions in the book of Psalms, it is unclear whether the psalmist is hoping to be rescued from Sheol in the sense of being brought back from Sheol, or in the sense of having the descent to Sheol indefinitely postponed. In either case, his hope is founded on the strong and permanent bond of affection that God has for his chosen ones. God so loves and protects them that he can never abandon any of them to see corruption.

4 O Lord, hear a cause that is just

Psalm 17 (16)

This confident prayer follows the previous psalm in much the same spirit, secure in the conviction that God will save, and also ending with a firm ex-pectation of final permanent company with the Lord: 'behold your face… with the vision of your presence' (v. 15). To see the face of the Lord is a bold way of expressing tranquil enjoyment of the divine presence. In the vision of the new Jerusalem with which the book of Revelation concludes, 'the throne of God and of the Lamb will be in the city; his servants will worship him; they will see him face to face' (Revelation 22:3–4).

One difference from the previous psalm is that, here, the psalmist is threatened by enemies. Indeed, it may be helpful to imagine him in the same situation as the prophet Jeremiah. Jeremiah was constrained to make himself unpopular as the Babylonian forces advanced to sack Jerusalem in 587BC. He graphically foretold the disaster that would follow if the na-tion continued in its stubborn refusal to return to the Lord, and was duly persecuted and imprisoned for his pains, being dumped in the mud of an almost-empty storage-well. The king had a good deal of sympathy for him, but was obviously constricted by his army officers and could help Jeremiah only secretly. The book of Jeremiah contains a series of poems in which Jeremiah complains to the Lord about the uncongenial task he has been given, protesting his loyalty but bemoaning the persecution it brings with it (for example, Jeremiah 20:7–18). This psalm similarly circles round the theme of confidence in divine protection against enemies who are pressing upon the psalmist.

The sequence of the psalm may be seen as fivefold, parts one, three and five being declarations of confidence in the Lord, each special in its way. So we see the structure:

Verses 1–2: Confidence in the Lord, based on 'my justice'. As we have noted, this is not a complacent protestation of perfect behaviour, but a trust in God's fidelity to his promises: Abraham trusted in God and this was accounted to him as justice.

Verses 3–5: A declaration of fidelity—by contrast to the violence of the enemy.

Verses 6–8: Confidence in the Lord. This is enthusiastic, almost wild. Verse 7a could be translated as an explosive 'Make a wonderful demonstration of your faithful love (hesed)'.

Verses 9–13: The enemy on the prowl, centred on the image of lions prowling round the camp at night, a blood-freezing experience.

Verses 14–15: Confidence in the Lord—the final face-to-face vision of God.

5 I love you, Lord my strength

Psalm 18 (17)

This is one of the longest of the psalms; in fact, only two are longer. Another feature is that it comes almost identically in an appendix to the story of David, in 2 Samuel 22. All the psalms were traditionally, of course, attributed to David, and most of them certainly falsely. Whether this one had David as its author or not, most of it nicely fits the life of David. Other divisions are possible, but to me it is most attractive to divide the psalm into two distinct halves, joined by the bridge of verses 20–24. This bridge itself is strongly reminiscent of the book of Deuteronomy, for it concentrates on observance of the Law ('the ways of the Lord', his 'judgments', 'blameless', 'kept from guilt', hands 'clean in his eyes'). The poems before and after are of a different stamp. The two halves are also connected at beginning and end by the strong stress on God as Rock (vv. 2 and 46), a dominant emphasis in each poem.

The first 19 verses form an energetic account of God's divine intervention, using the traditional Canaanite language and imagery of God as a deity of storm and nature. Baal, the chief god of Canaan before Israel's arrival, is always represented as a storm-god, hurling a thunderbolt. This is the imagery also of the divine encounter on Sinai, when the appearance of God to Moses and the Israelites is described in terms of thunder, lightning and earthquake (Exodus 19:16–18). At least in a world without explosives or nuclear fission, these were the most awesome manifestations of power imaginable. The uncontrollable force of hurricanes, tornados and tsunamis is irresistible even against modern precautions. They remain the most powerful image of the divine might. In the first 20 verses, this is the irresistible might that seizes David and saves him. Perhaps it might be considered a poetic commentary on the divine intervention in David's contest with Goliath.

The final section (vv. 25–50) is a vigorous celebration of how God—again as Rock—equipped and trained the psalmist as a victorious warrior. Today we would not perhaps celebrate with such gusto how the warrior crushed his enemies 'fine, like dust before the wind' (v. 42, NRSV). More suitable would be to adopt the Pauline application of the language of the Roman gladiatorial contests—the contemporary equivalent of football matches—to the armour of God in Ephesians 6:13–17.

6 The heavens declare the glory of God

Psalm 19 (18)

At first sight, this psalm consists of two independent psalms, one about the heavens, the other about the Law of the Lord. As is obvious, they are in different rhythms and lengths of line. However, it is also attractive to see the psalm as one continuous threefold whole: God speaks through the glory of the heavens; the Lord speaks through his revelation of the Law; the believer speaks in response.

The opening section of the psalm celebrates, first, the heavens declaring the glory of God by their unlimited expanse. Especially with our modern knowledge of the vast distances of space and the ever-expanding universe, it is impossible to look up at the night skies without being overawed by the Creator or without appreciating the littleness of the human race. Then the psalm celebrates the sun, rising and traversing the heavens. Today we might not celebrate the sun in just these terms, yet we cannot but be aware of the beneficent influence exerted by it and of our dependence on it. Contrast a cold and perishing world without the sun! In the first line of the psalm, the word for 'God' is 'El', the common word for a god; here we are celebrating the natural creation. In the second section of the psalm, the name will be YHWH, Israel's own special name for Israel's God. In verses 7–14 it is repeated seven times, the perfect number.

The second section of the psalm celebrates the special revelation of God to Israel, given in the Law, by which YHWH gives Israel both life and wisdom. The Law given to Israel on Sinai is not constricting but is liberating, for it shows how Israel may live as God's people, in the image of God and representing God to the world. They are shown the way to 'be holy as I am holy' (Leviticus 19:2). They are shown how to respect, revere and love the glory of God ('the fear of the Lord is pure', Psalm 19:9). They are shown how to respect and give dignity and life to other human beings ('You will treat resident aliens as though they were native-born and love them as yourself—for you yourselves were once aliens in Egypt', Leviticus 19:34). This is why the precepts of the Lord are more to be desired than gold, and sweeter than honey.

In the final verse, after the heavens have spoken of the glory of God, after God has revealed himself by speaking his Law, the psalmist asks that his own words may win favour with God, his Rock.

Guidelines

A feature of this group of psalms has been that most of them are private prayers, rather than prayers for public assemblies or prayers reflecting on God's care of Israel throughout history. Repeatedly God is hailed as 'my Rock', 'my Refuge'. Basically, prayer is a personal and private matter, an intimate love affair, in which we open ourselves to God's love and God nourishes our relationship to him, drawing us close to himself and revealing himself to us in the silence of our inmost being.

Let one or more of these psalms guide and inspire you in your own prayers today.

1 May the Lord answer in time of trial

Psalm 20 (19)

This psalm is often considered a coronation psalm. The first six verses are good wishes or congratulations to the king, rather than prayers. The last four verses express confidence in the Lord's patronage of the king, his anointed.

Scholars have attempted to pinpoint a particular king, the most likely focus being upon Josiah, although Josiah is only one possibility. He was king of Judah from 640 to 609BC, at the time of the Babylonian threat which was to destroy Jerusalem a decade after his death. This would account for the suggestion of danger in verse 1, 'in time of trial', and the assertions of confidence of victory in war. More persuasive is the insistence on the power of the name of the Lord (vv. 1, 5, 7). At this time, the time of the Deuteronomic reform under Josiah, there was considerable stress on the name of the Lord, standing for the power of the Lord. The name of the Lord is itself glorious and awe-inspiring (Deuteronomy 28:58). The Lord has placed his name to dwell in the temple of Jerusalem, meaning that his power is accessible there. However, a stress on the power of the name of the Lord is not confined to this period.

The psalm brings to mind the stress on the power of the name of the Lord Jesus in the New Testament and Christian context. Throughout Acts, Christians are baptised into the name of Jesus—that is, into the company of Jesus. All who call on the name of the Lord will be saved, says Peter at Pentecost (Acts 2:21). The followers of Jesus are known as those over whom the name of the Lord has been invoked or pronounced—fittingly, indeed, as they are known as 'Christians'. It is in the name of Jesus that Peter acts and works miracles (Acts 3:6). The name of Jesus designates the power in which Christians act more than 30 times in the Acts of the Apostles. This has become the equivalent of the name of the Lord in the Old Testament.

The other key word that occurs three times in the second half of the psalm is 'salvation' (v. 6: 'the Lord saves his anointed… with the mighty salvation of his right hand'; v. 9: 'Grant salvation to the king, O Lord').

In the original, this was no doubt understood in terms of military deliverance. In Christian prayer, however, it will bear a wider sense, meaning the salvation for which we long and for which we rely on the Lord. Salvation from sickness? From the evil tendencies of which I am ashamed? From anything I fear? From myself? Any earthly salvation is a pale shadow of this ultimate gift.

2 In your strength, O Lord, the king rejoices

Psalm 21 (20)

Like the previous psalm, this is a prayer for the king, though it has less emphasis on the actual coronation for it assumes that the king has already received the Lord's blessings. The structure may be regarded as twofold, verses 1, 7 and 13 being perhaps choral responses, while the intervening two sets of verses reflect on the blessings which the Lord has granted. The first set (vv. 2–6) reflects on his personal blessings, the second (vv. 8–12) on his military victories.

How should Christians pray this psalm in an age when the idea of war conjures up not merely individual heroism but death by 'friendly fire', mass destruction of civilians and other brutalising factors? Many, probably most, Christians would accept war as a very last resort, on the condition that the injustices and infringements of human rights it entails are less than in the alternative. In the Bible, wars, and even the slaughtering of enemies, are taken for granted. The most blood-chilling example is the slaughter of the prisoner-of-war Agag by Samuel in cold blood 'before the Lord' in 1 Samuel 15:33. War is, perhaps, the most extreme case of the gradual revelation and refinement of moral sensibilities. Just as truths about the relationship of God to human beings, in such matters as life after death, become clear only gradually, so do the moral teachings about how human beings should behave to one another. The Old Testament limited revenge: 'an eye [only] for an eye, and a tooth [only] for a tooth' (Exodus 21:24). In the Sermon on the Mount, Jesus bans revenge altogether (Matthew 5:39). The Old Testament permitted divorce and remarriage for 'fornication' (Deuteronomy 24:1), but Jesus bans it altogether (Mark 10:5–9).

Even the moral teaching of the New Testament on the love, respect and freedom due to each individual was, for many centuries, not seen by Christians as incompatible with slavery or forcible conversion. In praying this psalm and others that glory in slaughter, we can only ask that the world of today may be spared the hideous injustices of war, and be thankful for the gentle pressure of the Holy Spirit that has led us to a deeper understanding of the implications of biblical teaching. It is, after all, already there in the creation story, where human beings were created in the image of God to further and complete God's creation, not to destroy it. They were lapped in the peace of the garden of Eden. Even there, the guidance of the Spirit was required, for there human beings were free to eat the fruit of the plants. Meat-eating comes in only after the flood (Genesis 9:3), though this is not generally understood to prohibit the eating of meat.

3 My God, my God, why have you forsaken me?

Psalm 22 (21)

This psalm has a very special place in Christian prayer and devotion, for it is the psalm whose first words come on the lips of Jesus in his last agony on the cross in the Gospels of Mark and Matthew. The evangelists draw attention also to the fulfilment of other passages in this psalm during the course of the passion narrative, such as verses 7–8 and 17–18. It has often been interpreted as a cry of despair, as though, under the weight of the sins of the world, Jesus felt himself utterly abandoned and cut off from his Father, God-forsaken in the fullest sense. This will not do, though, for the crucifixion is the moment when Jesus is most fully united to his Father in perfect love. It is the loving obedience of Jesus in accepting the Father's will that undoes the disobedience of Adam. As Paul shows in Romans 5, the obedience of the second Adam annuls and reconciles the disobedience of the first Adam (for 'Adam' means 'man' or 'humanity' as a whole). It is this filial obedience that leads the centurion to say, 'Truly, this man was Son of God' (Mark 15:39).

Understood in its context, this cry of Jesus should be seen not in isolation but as the intonation of the whole psalm, the beginning of the psalm which gives the whole sense of the passion of Jesus. This is reinforced from time to time by the other quotations from the psalm in the passion narrative. The psalm moves through the desolation and humiliation of the sufferer to the glory to God and the triumphant recognition of the sufferer. It is only through suffering and desolation that the servant of the Lord achieves not only the glory of God but also his personal vindication and triumph. Jesus' intonation of the first verse of the psalm shows that this is the spirit in which he underwent the cross, confident in the glory of God and his own vindication. God the Father 'will rescue my soul from the sword' (v. 20) and 'they shall praise the Lord, those who seek him' (v. 26). Such confidence did not, of course, lessen the suffering, but it gave the suffering a purpose.

This psalm is often called 'The Psalm of the Suffering Servant' from its similarity to the Song of the Suffering Servant in Isaiah 53. By his allusion to this song at the last supper (his blood 'poured out for many'), it is clear that Jesus saw himself as this Servant of the Lord, who came 'not to be served but to serve, and to give his life a ransom for many' (Matthew 20:28).

4 The Lord is my shepherd

Psalm 23 (22)

There is an interesting and artistic balance in this psalm, of the pattern a-b-b-a. The first three verses reflect on the Lord as shepherd; then verse 4 addresses the Lord as shepherd directly, in the second person ('you'). In the latter half, the order is reversed: first the Lord is addressed directly ('you') as host, then the last verse is a further reflection on the Lord's welcome into his house.

The image of the shepherd gives the tone to this psalm, though by the third stanza the image has changed to the Lord as host, entertaining and comforting his guest. We like to think of sheep as frisky, cuddly lambs, but—like most of us—as they get older they get more difficult! Sheep are notoriously unpredictable, apt to dash helplessly across the road in front of any car, vulnerable, confused and in need of the most elementary guidance. In the steep valleys and rocky canyons of the Judean countryside, all too often one comes across the carcase of a sheep that went astray and ended up in the valley of the shadow of death.

In the countryside imagery of the Gospels, sheep are a favourite, and this may serve as a commentary on the psalm. Perhaps the best-known passage is the parable of the lost sheep. This is applied by Matthew (18:12–15) to teach the duty of the Christian to search out and bring back any member of the community who has strayed, and by Luke (15:4–7) to teach the exhilarating joy of forgiveness. The image is used in the only parable in the Gospel of John, that of the good shepherd (10:1–6). Here the generous love of Jesus' sacrifice, his devotion to the sheep who 'know his voice', is the point. It even distorts the image, for it is hardly an appropriate sacrifice of a shepherd to die for a sheep—presumably leaving the others untended.

A further use of the image is in the story of the feeding of the five thousand, and this even brings in the aspect of the Lord as host. Jesus begins by taking pity on the crowds 'because they were like sheep without a shepherd' (Mark 6:34). Then he feeds them on the green pastures beside the restful waters of the Sea of Galilee. This is the perfect picture of the shepherd giving food to his sheep, made more perfect by the eucharistic overtones of the piece. The Eucharist is always a gathering of Jesus and his disciples, and here we see the shepherd feeding his sheep as Jesus feeds his followers at the eucharistic table.

5 The Lord's is the earth and its fullness

Psalm 24 (23)

A possible opinion is that this psalm was written for a liturgical procession of the ark of the covenant into the temple, perhaps annually. The first half would then be a sort of examination of conscience, not unlike Psalm 15 (14), about who is worthy to participate in the procession, and the second half would be a liturgical lyric for the procession. The principal difficulty with this interpretation is that there is no suggestion anywhere that such a procession took place. Nor is the ark mentioned in this psalm. We know only that David brought the ark up to Jerusalem in the generation before the temple was built.

A clear feature of the psalm is the use of elevated language and myth. The opening verse invokes the story of creation, which sees the world as planted on pillars in the waters of chaos, sustained and held firm in those swirling and formless waters only by the continuously restraining hand of the Creator. From there we go on to the 'holy mountain', the mountain of the Lord, where the Lord is to be encountered—another mythical feature. Similarly, the 'ancient doors' are no ordinary doors; the phrase could be translated 'eternal doors' or 'doors of eternity'.

'The Lord of hosts' (v. 10) is a mysterious phrase which has never been wholly explained, but it probably refers to the heavenly hosts, the mythical astral deities and heavenly powers, over which the Lord is still in control. Even more, the 'King of glory' is no ordinary king. The phrase evokes the divine glory, something so holy and awesome as to be almost beyond the power of speech. Once Moses has experienced it, his face is horned or calloused (Exodus 34:30: a possible translation of the word usually rendered 'radiant' or 'shining') and he has to wear a veil over his face to protect others from the glare. Elijah wraps his face in his cloak to cope with his experience of the divinity in the daunting 'voice of silence' (1 Kings 19:12–13). The prophet Isaiah, at his vocation-vision of the glory of the Lord in the temple, shrinks away and cries out that he is a man of unclean lips (Isaiah 6:5). The only fitting reaction at the approach of the glory of the Lord is to hide in the rocks in terror of the Lord, at the brilliance of his majesty (a repeated refrain in Isaiah 2:10, 19, 21).

In sum, therefore, the psalm is a celebration in poetic and mythical terms of the daunting holiness of the Lord, and the unworthiness of human beings to associate with that holiness. Yet some are invited to climb the holy mountain of the Lord. We must do so in trepidation and reverence.

6 To you, O Lord, I lift up my soul

Psalm 25 (24)

This is the first of the acrostic psalms. English poetry often receives its form and balance from a rhyme at the end of the line. Hebrew poetry, on the other hand, often receives it from the letters of the alphabet at the start of the line. In this psalm, the verses begin successively with each of the letters of the Hebrew alphabet. The same structure occurs in other psalms, such as 34, 111 and 112. Psalm 119 is a special tour de force: each verse of the eight-verse sections begins with a successive letter of the alphabet.

The acrostic pattern seems to be a feature of post-exilic poetry. Such a date for this psalm would also fit the spirituality of the period, with its consciousness of guilt and failure and its eagerness for instruction in complete observance of God's pleasure.

The shape of the psalm is concentric. At the outside is an envelope (vv. 2–3 and 20–21): the psalmist's trust and hope is in the Lord, so he should not be put to shame. In the central part of the psalm, two themes interweave:

• The theme of instruction in the ways of the Lord, so that the psalmist may fulfil the covenant (vv. 4–5, 8–9, 12–14). Here, words like 'teach', 'guide', 'paths' and 'ways' predominate.
• The theme of forgiveness (vv. 6–7, 15–19). Here, the dominant words are 'mercy' (hesed) and 'compassion'.

At the very centre come verses 10–11, where the two themes are combined—instruction in the way, and forgiveness for failure. Both of these, the plea for guidance and the need for forgiveness, are valuable topics also for Christian prayer.

Guidelines

This week's psalms offer us a variety of subjects for prayer. In starting with two hymns for the king, we are reminded that kingship in Israel is the maintenance of the royal line of kings that will issue in the Lord's anointed Messiah, whose whole vision and perspective was to bring to reality the kingship or sovereignty of God in the world. This aspect is strengthened by the two psalms of the suffering servant and the good shepherd, whose imagery is so close to the central Christological themes of the New Testament. Finally, Psalm 24 renews our sense of the mystery and elevation of the divinity whom we dare to approach, and Psalm 25 brings us back to the daily concerns of our own moral lives and our need for forgiveness.

The gift of reconciliation

'Reconciliation' is a word from which the value is draining, as it loses its very deep roots and becomes an expression for a quick fix that stops an argument. A politician announces news of an initiative for reconciliation in the Middle East and, a week later, some political correspondent is asking why it has not been achieved. The idea that reconciliation is deeply costly, extremely lengthy and often uncertain gets lost in the rush of credit claiming. In areas of civil conflict, it often seems that everyone has an NGO (non-governmental organisation) working on reconciliation. Government programmes fund it; even commercial companies make money out of it.

All three of the Abrahamic faiths involve ideas of reconciliation, through the mercy of God, through sacrifice and through personal decision. For Christians, however, reconciliation is at the very heart of the gospel; indeed, it is often described as the absolute centre of the gospel. In the Catholic tradition, the sacrament of confession is now called the sacrament of reconciliation. Yet the church is extremely bad at it. From the local to the global, Christians argue with an intemperance that would be absurd if it were not so tragic. A national Sunday newspaper had a headline above a leading article on sexuality and the church: 'How these Christians hate one another'.

So these notes will take a brief and doubtlessly inadequate look at what we mean by reconciliation and what we should expect from it. We will think about issues of disagreement, of the personal and the corporate, of our role and vocation to be peacemakers, and of the source of reconciliation and its fount, the gracious and overwhelming love of God in Jesus Christ.

8–14 November

1 Forgiving and being forgiven

Luke 6:35–38

There is an intense link between reconciliation with God and our own acts of reconciliation and forgiveness, and it is in Luke, above all, that the link is pressed home in an extremely uncomfortable way. Grace is free, but not unconditional. The sign of the genuine reception of God's grace in our own lives is that there is an overflow to others. Professor David Ford at Cambridge talks of flourishing as Christians and as a Christian community (*Self and Salvation: Being Transformed*, CUP, 1999), and links flourishing to the overwhelming of ourselves by God. To be the object of God's grace should be utterly overwhelming, leading to far more than we can contain. Jesus very explicitly links our enjoyment of forgiveness, and of the generosity of forgiveness, to our willingness to be forgivers.

The importance of this is often ignored. Forgiving is treated as a good thing, desirable—but not essential. By his linking of horizontal and vertical forgiveness, however, Jesus sets the basis for reconciliation as part of our Christian ministry in the world, as well as part of our experience of God. This is where the bite comes: we receive what we give. The good measure is packed in. The experience of the forgiveness of God is literally life-transforming, and so is the experience of forgiveness between enemies or those who have fallen out. Today's passage comes in Luke's Sermon on the Plain, as the tension with the religious leaders is beginning to build. The shadow of the cross is over these words. They are not lightly spoken or received.

There is a temptation to be dismayed by all this. When we come to realise the extent of God's forgiveness, and the fact that we can cut ourselves off from the knowledge of divine forgiveness by rejecting the call to forgive, we might start to think, 'I can't do it!' Our family experience of the death of a child, and my own experience of working for five years in areas of war on issues of conflict, have led me to be careful about cheap exhortations to forgive. We will be exploring more of the 'how' next week, but forgiving and being forgiven starts with a recognition of broken relationship with oneself, or in the church, or with God, and a prayer that I might at least want something better.

2 Reconciling and being reconciled

Matthew 6:22–34

We have looked at the fact that God does reconcile, and his reconciliation is linked to our cooperation in overflowing with reconciliation to the world. Reconciliation with God is the root of all human reconciliation; from him we receive the power and capacity to be reconciled and to reconcile. Reconciliation is something that deals with the roots of problems, not merely the symptoms. So much of what we call 'reconciliation' is not renewed relationship at a deep level, but simply the ending of open violence or hostility. Strife is based, above all, on power and desire for power, and desire for power is very often rooted in insecurity.

In this passage, we are called to a reconciliation with contingency, with the uncertainty and unpredictability of life. It seems to be one of those counsels of perfection, yet it begins with the image of light and wholeness, themselves the result of reconciliation. We kid ourselves about the light within us, which is seen in truth only by God. His light shines when we belong to him. The passage is not saying that poverty is good but that futile striving for the temporary, a sour highest priority, is foolish, and foolishness leaves us in darkness. We are called to strive, but for the permanent; our reconciliation with God makes that possible and, better still, makes the very act of such striving into an act that heals.

In 1974, Archbishop Van Thuan, the Roman Catholic Archbishop of Saigon (as it was), was arrested after the victory of the communist north. Taken to prison to begin 13 years of suffering, he was stripped of clothes, name, rank and purpose. Put on a ship sailing north, he was surrounded by people in the depths of contagious despair. He testified of God saying to him, 'Now you have only me'—and of that being enough.

3 Reconciliation across boundaries

Ephesians 2:11–22

The overflow of reconciliation is set out most beautifully in this passage. It is a poem of transformation, in which what happens with the individual and God, with the believing community and God, and with different human communities and traditions, are all mixed into a cocktail of reconciliation. It is dependent on the wonderful combination of God's gracious reaching to us in forgiveness and our response in letting grace flow to others. It is embedded in a life that lays aside seeking for power and, thus, the concerns of uncertainty, and the result is the new people of Ephesians 2.

Bishop Sandy Millar once commented that 'the miracle of the church is not that like-minded people love one another, but that the most unlike-minded do'. It is hard to exaggerate the radicality of this passage. Jews and Gentiles were separated physically in the Jerusalem temple by a wall that it was death for a Gentile to cross. They were separated by rules of ritual and by hatred and suspicion in many areas. To suggest that the death of Jesus had removed these divisions was to turn the world upside down.

The trouble is, we agree, we get used to the idea and we ignore it. An American friend described Sunday morning as the most segregated three hours of the week, as different racial groups in the USA attend different churches. He talked of the difficulty he encountered in his liberal, Episcopalian church when he suggested that they work jointly with some of the local black congregations. It's not that different in the UK. In the holy land, the divisions of war separate Christians of different backgrounds. Class is another barrier—and, of course, theology. Living in Liverpool, the idea that we work closely with the Roman Catholics is so normal that it is easy to forget how radical it was 30 years ago.

Reconciliation across boundaries is a gift achieved by God, and it needs appropriating by conscious effort, which is what Paul is encouraging the Ephesians to make. For the church to be the body of reconciled reconcilers that shines a light in the world, each of us needs to look at the places where we have rebuilt walls.

4 Acceptable confrontation

Galatians 2:1–14

Rebuilding walls through fear, habit and culture is nothing new. Peter was building hard when Paul challenged him. The radicality of the idea that reconciliation with God is for all people was foreseen in the Old Testament, but theory and practice are different. It was a problem from the earliest days of the Church (see Acts 6), and never went away. In pessimistic moments, we might argue that by the end of the first century Christians and Jews had withdrawn into mutual incomprehension and hostility, which still exists, undoing the achievement of the cross in breaking down barriers. It is easy to go along with a settling back into old patterns, and perhaps one of the marks of the great saints was that they refused to do so. They were constrained by the love of Christ more than by the traditions they inherited.

So what do we do when it all seems to be going wrong? Paul tackles the situation head-on and challenges Peter. We don't really know the outcome. Most of us avoid confrontation and, instead, seethe and grumble. The result is not often inspiring in terms of reconciled reconcilers. The essence of the issue was the right understanding of scripture (in their case, what we call the Old Testament) and its impact on the inclusion of those whose lifestyle and heritage were not according to traditional Jewish customs. In other words, it really mattered. Reconciliation among Christians does not have unanimity at its heart, or tolerance, but the capacity to love despite disagreement, and to differ and be diverse without breaking fellowship. The difficulty is where to draw the boundaries and decide that a difference is of such fundamental importance that a breakdown of fellowship is necessary. It is worth noting that Paul does not go that far, even on this issue; he confronts but does not divide. Yet at moments of confrontation, our anger (albeit justified) can push us past acceptable behaviour.

Looking at this passage, I wonder how I would behave in this situation. If I were Paul, would I perhaps make excuses for Peter, drawing back from confrontation, or even splitting off to form my own new congregation? If I were Peter, would I hit back at Paul, ending up by breaking fellowship with him? What is there to learn here about acceptable confrontation?

5 Cosmic reconciliation

Romans 8:18–25

Power is most easily abused when it is wielded over those who can't or won't answer back, where there is a complete imbalance of power. The more that power is abused, the less reconciliation can flow. If there had been a balance of power among the Galatians, it would have made confrontation a little easier.

At the heart of the gospel is the extraordinary miracle of the self-emptying of power and privilege that is the incarnation. In this very remarkable and short passage, Paul goes cosmic on reconciliation. There is no suggestion that Paul was in any way a first-century environmentalist. That would be a ridiculous anachronism. But he sees the issue of the cosmic sin of

Adam faced and overcome by the cosmic reconciliation of Christ, with the whole of creation caught up in this movement towards restoration. Of all abuses of power, humanity's abuse of the creation is increasingly seen as both the most pervasive and the most destructive, threatening our very existence. Creation does not answer back directly but responds through symptoms of abuse—disintegration, systemic change and such like.

Yet, such is the overflow of reconciliation, so lavish the provision of God, that it explodes into the whole of creation as a force of liberation. There is so much to think about here. Firstly, to be reconciled is to be freed from frustration, constraints and decay, for a journey of hope to a destination of glory. Practically, we should find that, in thankfulness, our own reconciliation overflows into our actions in the world around us, in creation itself. Secondly, the sense of doom and inevitability that overcomes us when reading some forecasts of climate change is not necessary, because creation is within the view and grasp of God and his reconciliation. Our responsibility remains, but our task is achievable. Thirdly, our own hope is all tied up with the reconciliation of creation; we hope in partnership with a creation itself tormented and groaning but also invaded by hope.

6 Reconciliation and justice

Revelation 21:1–8

Over the last few years, I have been much involved with long-term issues of reconciliation, from local churches through to civil wars. Each of them is unique, but one aspect common to all conflict is that waves of issues are embedded in immense complexity. Just puzzling out what is going on is usually impossible. The temptation is to get bogged down in the short term and lose sight of the eventual outcome that we are seeking. We try to get through the next meeting, and fail to hold to a vision of a functional and peaceful society. At the political level, this leads to 'declarationitis', the disease of making declarations and concluding that by doing so we have changed the world. It is as though, by some strange semiotic mechanism, talking enough about reconciliation can lead to its happening.

God's lavish gift does not work like that. The book of Revelation is, to put it mildly, a challenging read, but this picture, well known to those involved in funerals, has a clear central theme—reconciliation completed. It matters because we need to see the destination towards which we are travelling. Reconciliation is effective but not universal in this picture. In most conflicts the toughest word is justice, because, until there is justice, reconciliation is constrained, and until there is some reconciliation, no one trusts much in justice. But in this passage we see the two put together. Reconciliation is not always effective for everyone; it requires response, and some are pictured as saying 'no'. Justice is too often divisive because it is too often victor's justice: only in God's hands is it truly just. It makes sense of the cost of reconciliation and stops it diluting into mere tolerance. At the same time, the reality of justice and the finalising of reconciliation in a just moment of renewal should make us reflect on our need for holiness, in order to be ready to welcome God's completed generosity.

Guidelines

In the last few days, I have tried to emphasise three things:

- Reconciliation is lavish and overwhelming and leads in the end to a wonderful human flourishing.
- It is two-way: we have to respond and keep responding to the unending flow of gracious reconciliation that is the work of God in Christ.
- It is costly and divisive because it necessarily includes justice.

It is worth spending a few minutes responding to these three aspects of reconciliation. We need to allow ourselves to be caught up in the stream, seeing its sufficiency for our weaknesses and failures and, indeed, for the failures of not only the church as a whole but for all of humanity. We need to reflect on our own response and giving of forgiveness and embedding of reconciliation in our lives—and I wince even as I write these words. We need to be content with accepting that not all will accept reconciliation, and thus not beat ourselves up over what even God's grace has not reached in full.

1 Spiritual disciplines

Luke 6:39–49

It is a very common experience to see someone projecting their own difficulties on to others. This is especially true when it comes to judging others. People are dismissed out of hand because of a sin or failing, and then it becomes clear that the person judging was struggling with the same sin. Jesus calls it hypocrisy, which has a root meaning of 'acting', 'putting on a face'. For reconciliation to overflow from us, it has to start within us. After that, the process is, in the mechanics of grace, almost automatic. But the question is, how?

Anyone who has any involvement in pastoral care knows that one of the most frequent issues to be found at the root of problems in a relationship is that one or both parties are unable to accept that God is forgiving and loving, not just in general but to them in particular. It's not just a question of going on telling oneself, or screwing up all one's spiritual strength and making it seem true. Many, perhaps most, Christians go around with a sense of inadequacy and guilt that can go as far as self-hatred, because they feel that they do not meet God's standards. The result is angst which is often projected on to others, or into illness and depression, or in judgmentalism and anger. This is what Jesus is reflecting in verses 43–45. Psychologically, what goes on inside us overflows to what we do to others.

There are no easy answers, but there are spiritual disciplines, and this is where they come in. The regular practice of self-examination in quietness and before God, perhaps with a journal, often enables a clearer recognition of what is within us. Depending on our tradition, the use of the sacrament of reconciliation, a spiritual director or a prayer partner with whom we can be honest in guaranteed confidentiality, all permit integrity and transparency before God, and thus open us to the work of his Spirit in our own acceptance of his reconciliation of ourselves. Regular corporate worship, reading scripture and prayer are essentials. With all these go the disciplines that Jesus calls for in verses 41–42. Although demanding, they are part of the effort of putting down the foundations that enable us to stand firm in the flood.

2 Church unity

John 17:20–26

Most of us should find this a really worrying passage. We are tempted to ask, if Jesus' own prayers are answered as little as this one appears to be, what chance is there for the rest of us? At a recent count, there were 36,000 denominations in the USA alone. Protestant churches are especially prone to division—always, of course, on points of principle. But look at Jesus' prayer and see the purpose of unity. It is so that the world will know that Jesus is from God (v. 21). The unity of his Church is one of the principal means of evangelism, of convincing people that Jesus is God, and that faith and salvation have content (vv. 20, 21, 23). Unity is also the means by which we experience the love of Christ in our midst. There are powerful echoes of the same thought at the end of Acts 2 and 4.

What, then, do we make of the absence of unity? Did the Father simply say 'no' to the prayer of Jesus? Or is the prayer platitudinous (or, at best, utopian) editorial imagination by the writer of the Gospel? As we saw with the need for spiritual discipline if we are to avoid hypocrisy, there are no short cuts to reconciliation in the Church, among Christians, but it is an absolute essential. To be one is not to be an indistinguishable lump but to be committed deeply to one another, respecting and loving one another profoundly. It is to seek to serve, not rule, and to follow the pattern of the relationship between the Father and the Son. If we take the reconciling work of Jesus seriously, we will take seriously the need to build up the unity of our own church groups and congregations, enabling peace through the overflow of our own reconciliation with God, and seeking to heal divisions. The chief tools in this work are affirmation and service. Affirmation in the church is the celebration of others' success, and service is seeking to enable that success without seeking our own place and position.

3 Who is our enemy?

Luke 6:27–36

Divine reconciliation is so lavish that it should overflow not only within the Church but also to our enemies. Regrettably, there is quite often a significant overlap between the two. 'Enemies' is a strong word. I have had a very few enemies when working in areas of civil conflict—people who, for one reason or another, wanted to kill me (the most notable case being when the person concerned was drunk and high; I wasn't glamorous enough to warrant really serious attention from a coldly sober enemy). Somehow, I have never had any trouble forgiving that, but how much more difficult it is with those closer to home who can become real enemies. I know of one cathedral where two of the clergy could not bear to be in the same room. There is the famous story of the politician making a maiden speech in the House of Commons. He was congratulated afterwards by an MP of many years' standing. 'Oh,' said the novice, 'I was very nervous with all my enemies looking at me from the opposition benches.' 'Oh no, lad,' said the older MP, 'the other party are your opponents; your enemies are in your own party.'

So the first thing to do when we are reading this passage is to be honest about who our enemies are. After all, we can't love them unless we identify them. The second thing is actively to seek not just to feel forgiving (which can be very hard indeed—feelings get out of control so easily) but to do good to them. Jesus is always severely practical. Pray for them; lend them money; help them to succeed where you can. In doing so, we will imitate God who is merciful to us, who has done all that is necessary for our reconciliation despite our ingratitude and sin, who is merciful. Is this a counsel of perfection? Perhaps, but it would make a very big difference if it was even tried within the Church. How much more impact it would have if Christians sought to do good for those who attack them more widely. Can we look for a way to seek good things for Professor Dawkins?

4 Reconciliation in communities

Galatians 5:16–26

Reconciliation begins within ourselves, it is lived out in the Church and, where there are functional church communities, reconciliation pours out from them into the world around. We see the effects in history. What might be called the 'fruit of the flesh' has so often spilled out of the Church into our politics and polities that Christian history is littered with corpses. By contrast, when the Church is at its best, the transformational impact on society is staggering. South Africa after 1991 is a breathtaking example of what can be achieved. Even before the fall of the apartheid regime, it was very often the church that led the way in reconciliation.

The fruit of the Holy Spirit is corporate, not individual. No one person shows all of its aspects: Paul is talking to a church and calling it to demonstrate the reality of the presence of God in its midst. Also, fruit is for picking. The towns and cities of Asia Minor and Greece where Paul worked were small by today's standards: think of a small market town in rural England. The reputation of the church would spread quickly and powerfully and arouse opposition, admiration or envy. One parish where I was involved in reconciliation work saw the need for it when jokes about their divisions started being made by the local hairdresser. That is the fruit of the flesh.

What is the fruit that our communities pick from us and consume? If it is the spiritual fruit of reconciliation, it will show itself in the life of our own area, even where that is a life of poverty and suffering. In Goma in the Democratic Republic of the Congo, this year, I saw the result of a loving community bearing fruit in a place of almost absolute poverty and strife. There were small efforts made against the challenge of a gigantic problem, but those small efforts lit up the darkness. Where, in our communities, are the points of stress at which the overflow of reconciliation would bring change and the savour of Christ?

5 Wise reconciliation

James 3:13–18

The metaphor of overflowing reconciliation can be pushed too far. Mere overflow, a sort of splodge of reconciliation, may or may not be helpful. James is speaking of wisdom, the capacity to make the right decision in the light of the nature of God, so that his purposes may be furthered. A colleague of mine was involved in hostage negotiation overseas. After several weeks, he had reached the point where the hostage takers were willing to surrender their captives. At that point, another group arrived from Europe and began a large-scale 'demonstration for peace'. In the midst of the resulting chaos, the hostages were lucky not to be killed, and it was another week before the situation could be stabilised and progress made. The new group were unrepentant. They had, in their opinion, drawn attention to the conflict and fulfilled their calling.

Wisdom that is from above produces peace, the sign of true reconciliation. As we saw earlier, it springs from purity of motive (v. 14, compare v. 17). There is no hint of self in it. It is inclusive (v. 17), seeking the good of all.

This sort of wisdom requires thought and preparation. We cannot rush blindly, ill-informed and uninformed, into conflicts, whether merely between individuals or within societies or communities. The key is our own motivation. Wise reconciliation leads to our being unknown and the harvest being visible (v. 18). It takes the preparation of listening to people caught up in conflict, the character that means they want to speak to us, and the determination to enable them to find their own way to an answer.

So where do we start? The answer is with building relationships, and not showing partiality but seeking to be merciful. From there, wisdom calls us to action, a response of meeting practical needs. If we are to reconcile, we must take the risk of being vulnerable, of being rejected. Finally, we must take time and have patience, being content for our part to be forgotten— which in all probability it will be, except by God.

6 Blessings and woes

Luke 6:20–26

The Sermon on the Plain is similar to the Sermon on the Mount, with some wrinkles. There are fewer Beatitudes, and there are woes. It is focused on the physical and economic (typical of Luke), and not so much on 'spiritual' terms. It is altogether much shorter. For me, it is more uncomfortable. It is Jesus' manifesto, his campaign strategy. Reading it, we find a passion about the people and a courage in facing the great unreconciled divisions of his time and ours. The poor were against the rich; those who mourned were uncomforted by those who rejoiced; those who obeyed God and sought to serve him were persecuted by those in authority. It is worth reflecting on who we would think of as being in each category today. There are moments when the sheer despair of a camp of internally displaced people seems unutterable faced with the acquisitiveness of an English Christmas, but that sentiment is often facile and clichéd, and we will all think of examples much closer to home.

Luke is not writing the words of Jesus to make us feel guilt, but to make us build bridges, and he tells us how to do that in the passages from later in the sermon that we have considered over the last couple of weeks.

So these blessings and woes should be a motivating force for us. They are to be meditated on, with integrity, not self-abnegation. Many people will be among those being 'blessed' and will not be entirely sure that they like the form of blessing. The reaction 'something must be done' is the one that sends armies to fight wars of liberation, which turn into campaigns of suffering for soldiers and inhabitants alike. The question is, 'What must I do, now?'

Guidelines

The Church has the answer to conflict, as a gift from God, its own experience and store of reconciliation. We can face the great issues of the world and have an answer. It is costly, dangerous and difficult. In one sense, God made the product, 'reconciliation', and holds the copyright. But he has given us each as individuals, and collectively as his people, a production licence. Just as people working in a chocolate factory are surrounded by its aroma, so we will be enveloped in the savour of reconciliation; but, unlike them, we will not become sick of the fragrance.

What does our own church community look like as an example of reconciled reconcilers? Is the production of reconciliation slight—just enough for some individuals, but rationed, measured out carefully and sparingly among rivalries and power struggles? Or is it ration-free, more than we can consume ourselves, so that we can spread it equally lavishly to our neighbours and communities and even into the wider world?

If I am honest, I don't think I have seen the latter on more than a very limited and small scale, but I have seen it and seen the effect. It is magnetic, but not effortless. St Benedict, in his Rule for monks, set a structure of common ownership, of work, prayer and rest, that led to reconciled communities in many cases (and not in many others, showing that there is no magic button). His formula revolves around stability of life, based on the gift of God's grace and obedience to one another, especially to superiors. It reflects the culture of the sixth century in some aspects (for example, the assumption of hierarchy, discipline and corporal punishment), combined with the practical application of reconciled life together. Its aim was to draw people close to Christ; its effect was to save the civilisation of Europe—protecting learning and literacy, encouraging the foundation of schools, hospitals and universities, and generally promoting the idea that human beings are at their best when pursuing virtue as disciples of Christ. Perhaps that is a measure of what God's gift of reconciliation can do.

In the first week, we looked at a very small aspect of what that gift is. In this second week, we have tried to look at how it can be our experience and calling to be reconciled reconcilers, so that when we share God's peace around his table, there is deep content to the action and the intention, and we bless the world in which we live.

FURTHER READING

Miroslav Volf, *Exclusion and Embrace: A Theological Exploration of Identity, Otherness and Reconciliation* (Abingdon Press, 1994).

Miroslav Volf, *Free of Charge: Giving and Forgiving in a Culture Stripped of Grace* (Zondervan, 2006).

Humour in the book of Esther

Biblical interpretation is always subjective. Numerous ways to approach and read the Bible lead to even more numerous interpretations of it. This multivalent aspect of the Bible is one of its most fascinating and exciting characteristics. The Bible continues to speak to us at different times, in different ways, in different life situations, in different voices, through different experiences, and on and on.

An interpretation project of mine over the last several years has been to read the Bible with eyes peeled for evidence there of humour, of comedy. Humans are blessed with the ability to experience the world through humour, yet we, as people of faith, often take a resolutely 'serious' approach to reading the Bible. Perhaps we think that comedy is too light a way to engage with so weighty a part of our lives. Perhaps we find in humour an attitude of disrespect that is unworthy of faith. Whatever the reason(s) we might pause over laughing in faith, we miss the mark when we equate the perception of humour in something with a lack of seriousness toward that something. Indeed, the multitude of satirical television and radio news quizzes reminds us that some of the most grave and weighty messages come to us with a twinkle in the eye, a smirk on the lips and laughter in the voice.

One biblical book in which people are most prone to agree that, yes indeed, there is some humour is the book of Esther. But then we reach the final chapters, the bodies start piling up and we are left thinking, 'This has just become so very unfunny.' The violence of Esther's final chapters is one of the reasons the book has struggled through the centuries to claim its rightful place as a widely read, taught, preached, discussed and appreciated biblical book. Yet, reading Esther as comedy all the way through the book, into the violence and beyond, overcomes the funny/unfunny bisection of Esther and opens up another avenue of interpretation for this story of a ridiculous king, a cruel politician and the two savvy and bold Jews who outwit them.

All biblical quotations are from the New Revised Standard Version and are taken from the book of Esther unless otherwise indicated.

1 The fateful party

Esther 1

An unrestricted, open-bar, 180-day bash topped off with a seven-day kingdom-wide shindig, held in an opulent palace… what more could any king desire? What, indeed, except to show off his queen to the boys like a 20-pound prize trout. But, unfortunately for Ahasuerus, this queen, Vashti, isn't biting. You wouldn't think a little word like 'no' could be enough to halt the party, send the king and his lawyers into a mad panic and necessitate the immediate adoption of a new law regarding that little word 'no' and the insolent women who wield it. In the court of Ahasuerus, 'over the top' is not just a way to throw a garden party; it is the way to rule a kingdom. Even as we may feel bad for Vashti, packing her bags to go, surely we are still giggling at the thought that her seemingly small act of defiance sent an entire kingdom and its 'wisest' men into a tailspin that, apparently, was solvable only through the codification of their superiority.

Hyperbole is one of the most often and effectively used tools of humour in the book of Esther. The book's opening verses, which describe the scene in such exaggerated detail, prepare the audience for all the exaggeration, inflation and overreaction that is to come. As will be seen time and again, Esther is drenched in hyperbole. A woman says 'no' to her husband and suddenly an entire kingdom is under threat. The reader is consistently reminded of a kingdom spanning 127 provinces (1:1; 5:3; 8:9). The opulence of the court and the extravagance of the 187-day drinking party are nauseatingly described (1:6–8). An indulgent king must have his pick from every beautiful young virgin in the kingdom (2:3). These potential queens require preparation before presentation—one whole year of scrubbing and soaking (2:12–14) for just one night (unless she really takes the king's fancy). Gallows built to the staggering height of 50 cubits (over 22 metres) are erected (5:14)! And finally the Jews show themselves to be fantastic killing, destroying, annihilating machines, taking out 75,800 of their enemies in only two days (9:12, 15–16).

Without the story ever needing to state it, a picture is drawn of this Persian reign under which the diaspora Jews are forced to live: a kingdom of excess, overindulgence, inefficiency, imprudence and foolish impulsiveness.

2 The Miss Persia pageant gets underway

Esther 2:1–11

When Ahasuerus finally sobers up from the partying and recovers from the unfortunate national security crisis, he realises that another crisis is before him: the kingdom has no queen! So the Miss Persia pageant commences, and at that point we first encounter Mordecai, the Jew, and his cousin/adopted daughter, Esther.

We can imagine the tender scene in which Mordecai gives Esther his final pearls of fatherly wisdom before sending her on her way to register for the pageant. 'I love you. I wish your parents could be here to see how wonderfully you've turned out. Your family and all your people are so proud of you. You take each of us with you in your heart. Never, ever forget who you are and where you come from. Now go, but just remember this: forget who you are and where you come from! No matter what, you are never, ever to tell a single soul who your people are!'

Important characteristics of comedy are its flexibility and adaptability. Comedy relishes compromising or even abandoning accepted norms and values if this abandonment serves a humorous purpose. Comedy, then, has no fixed moral code. Its ethics are not absolute: they conform to the situation at hand. It would help Esther's chances of becoming a foreign queen if her subjects (and, indeed, her husband) had no inkling that she was foreign.

Esther's strategy of withholding the truth of her identity stands in direct contrast to that of Daniel, Shadrach, Meshach and Abednego (Daniel 1; 3), who, in similar political situations, openly defied the reigning power on the basis that they were being asked to act against their religious beliefs. According to the Bible, then, Esther's approach to living in diaspora is one way, but not the only way. When in 'foreign' surroundings, along a spectrum from complete assimilation to complete rejection, Esther and Daniel represent choices at either end. While Esther's choice might cause some moral discomfort, comedy releases us from this dilemma, encouraging those of us who are in on the joke to smirk at the cleverness of Mordecai and Esther.

3 A winner is (finally) crowned

Every one of the kingdom's beautiful virgins is undergoing a year's preparation for one night with the king: it's no wonder the Miss Persia pageant has been underway for *four years* (1:3; 2:16) when a winner is finally awarded her crown. Again, we encounter the book's hyperbolic style of storytelling.

This derisive exaggeration is meant to mock the Persians and the way the kingdom is governed. 'Making fun' of an 'other' creates boundaries between 'us' and 'them', and this boundary-drawing is one of comedy's primary functions. Humour's divisions draw a line around one group (me and those like me), leaving another group (them and those like them) on the outside of the boundary. Comedy draws 'us' into the circle, while simultaneously drawing 'them' outside it.

The boundaries drawn in Esther are clear: on one side are the pompous, officious, foolish Persians and on the other are the savvy, courageous, intelligent Jews. 'Foreigners' are frequent interlopers into the story of the nation of Israel. Egyptians, Canaanites and Persians are a few that feature prominently. It follows, then, that these 'others' are frequent butts of the Israelite joke. Another notable example is the Egyptian pharaoh in Exodus who is completely duped by two lowly Hebrew midwives (Exodus 1:15–21).

The nation of Israel saw itself as being in a special, unchanging relationship with Yahweh, which no other people could enjoy in quite the same way. Their circle was tightly and deeply drawn between them and those nations that did not fear or follow Yahweh. The comic elements in the stories of the Israelites, then, frequently serve to accentuate this self-understanding as a nation over and against 'other' nations.

This encircling nature of comedy goes beyond simply a demarcation. In circumstances when 'they' gain control and threaten 'us', comedy has the further capacity, through the diminishment of 'them', also to diminish 'their' dominion. Thus comedy's 'making fun' helps to manage the threat, fear, and uncertainty that accompany the situation of being under the thumb of an 'other'. Comedy becomes a subversive force, working to dethrone the foreign power. In making 'them' a laughing stock, the Israelites take aim at and bring down the ruling powers—if not literally and permanently, certainly in no less powerful a way.

And so the subversive comedy of the Old Testament brings us the book of Esther, where we meet Ahasuerus, the fool king, and Esther, who manipulates and dupes him, in the process saving her people, the Israelites.

4 The idiot king

Esther 3

Comedy's flat characters can usually be summed up in one word. Ahasuerus = fool (or idiot or buffoon or clown). Haman = villain (or knave or braggart). These stock character types can be relied upon to act and react the same way every time: they are simple characters with a single characteristic or a repeated response that becomes their defining trait.

Esther offers us a quartet of characters, heroes and buffoons, who play off and against one another to create much of the humour. Haman's complete infuriation at Mordecai's refusal to do obeisance to him can be relied upon like the sunrise and paying VAT, just as can Mordecai's refusal to do obeisance to Haman without regard for the consequences. We can imagine Haman spluttering and red-faced as Mordecai winks to the audience in an aside that begs our silent collusion in his defiance.

Thus, in one pair we have a villain and a hero—the former seemingly with the fate of the latter in his hands; the latter completely disdainful of the power of the former. This single but repeated interaction between Haman and Mordecai is the event that spins out of control, so that the fate of a people hangs in the balance.

In another pair, we have the foolish king and the villainous adviser—comedy's ubiquitous fool and the villain who manipulates him. Ahasuerus seems never to have had a governing-related thought of his own. Enter his ministers, Haman at their forefront, ever ready themselves to plant those thoughts in the frivolous head of state. Ahasuerus is the idiot king, a jester in his own court, and Haman is the knave, using the king to get his own personal agenda decreed as national policy. Ahasuerus is too occupied with parties and virgins and losing his head around his queen to realise that, even as he offers her half his kingdom merely upon the sight of her, he has already and quite literally signed her death warrant. Ahasuerus is the idiot king.

5 A hidden God or a determined duo?

Esther 4

In addition to its violence, another reason why Esther has been difficult for its audience over time is that it lacks the expected Old Testament references. The book makes no mention of worship, Torah, Jerusalem, religious practices or any similar, regularly occurring Old Testament theological themes. Most significantly, the book of Esther lacks any reference to God.

Readers of the text have widely clung to Mordecai's words to Esther, 'Who knows? Perhaps you have come to royal dignity for such a time as this' (4:14b), finding in these words a reference to God—a hidden God working behind the scenes, a God who does know and who has some plan that is falling into place.

Yet comedy embraces hiddenness and the inevitable surprise that it eventually brings when what was hidden is now revealed. Comedy does not require God to be present, on the scene or behind the scenes, in order for it to do its work of telling the story.

Also, while it may feel more comforting and theologically satisfying to understand God as present, albeit hidden, in this story, not only does comedy not require it but nor does the Old Testament demand it. Esther and Mordecai, acting together in difficult circumstances and doing the best they can with whatever resources they have, stand alongside a number of other figures of the Old Testament—Abraham and Sarah, Tamar, Ruth and Naomi, to name a few. These figures are ones who, with better or worse results, act in seemingly desperate situations in the best ways they know how, without awaiting or even appearing to expect intervention from God. Furthermore, they are ultimately not condemned for their actions, not by the text and not by God. Indeed, in each case—eventually—their actions lead to a good result, a lasting one.

So, despite the instinct to understand Esther and Mordecai as acting in accordance with some divine plan being overseen by a hidden God, other Old Testament stories would concur with comedy on this one. Esther and Mordecai mobilised themselves in a desperate situation, using the tools they had to hand, without waiting for direct divine intervention. And they were able, in so doing, to save their people from being killed, destroyed and annihilated.

6 Other hidden things

As discussed in relation to the previous reading, hiddenness and the future surprise it promises are integral parts of comedy. Who knows what and when, who is being kept in the dark and for how long, when and how they might finally be let in on the joke: all these concealments and revelations combine to create confusion, heightened expectation and, ultimately, hilarity.

The most significant hidden factor in the comedy of Esther is Esther's 'secret' identity as a Jew. Mordecai instructs Esther to keep her secret, and twice the audience is reminded that she has faithfully done so (2:10, 20). But surely, despite Esther's diligence, someone, some time, ought to have figured it out, because her path crosses the path of Mordecai (who is well known to be a Jew—just ask Haman) way too often for the connection to be anything innocent. He is her sponsor in the Miss Persia pageant, and his 24/7 hangout appears to be the palace. He's there checking up on Esther; he's there being an irritant to Haman; he's there overhearing assassination plots. Esther brings news of the assassination plot to the king 'in the name of Mordecai' (2:22). Finally, the pair of them have a (hopefully fit) eunuch running back and forth between them, shuttling clothes and messages, as they work out their course of action after the sending of Haman's 'kill, destroy, annihilate' decree. Only in this kingdom ruled over by an idiot and a court full of over-reactive fools would the powers-that-be miss these flashing neon signs saying that Esther is Jewish. Esther's success at remaining hidden is just one more exclamation mark over the obliviousness and ineptitude of the king and his court.

In today's passage, we see that Esther has learned well from Mordecai the benefits of keeping certain details to oneself. In inviting only the king and Haman to her banquet, she outwardly appears to be honouring them, hiding her true motivation from the king and the for-the-time-being blissful and blissfully ignorant Haman. However, we too are partly in on this particular secret. While Esther's exact plan is still known only to her, we do know that she has now launched her scheme to intervene with the king on behalf of her people, and we clap our hands in anticipation of how it will all play out. We are also beginning to hear, just faintly in the distance, the rising chimes of doom for Haman as well.

Guidelines

Two points raised this week deserve our particular reflection as Christians living in this time. The first point is raised by the difference between the way the characters in Esther and those in Daniel try to survive life under foreign rule. The former choose assimilation, while the latter choose rejection, and all the characters thrive as a result of their choices. A relevant question for us, then, is about how far we go to become indistinguishable from the culture that surrounds us, versus how far we go to separate ourselves completely from it. How much ought we to put our Christianity on display, so to speak, and when might we keep our beliefs concealed from those around us? The Old Testament offers more than one response to this question, so we are left, yet again, without the simple answer we may sometimes desire. We must, it seems, continue asking ourselves and God what is our best response, while at the same time attempting to live faithfully as challenges from the culture in which we live present themselves before us.

The second point is closely related to the first and arises from the quest to locate God in the story of Esther. We desire and seek God's presence with us, but at times God does seem hidden—or even absent and indifferent. Yet we learn from Esther, and others of her Old Testament family, an incredibly inspiring lesson. We too can, in challenging times, do our best with what tools and resources we have at our disposal, and we can have a real hope that eventually we will see a good result from that effort. The Bible gives a rich and diverse portrayal of a God who can, will and does intervene. It also portrays a God who appears content for us quite simply to get on with it the best we can, if we are ready and willing to do so, and if we have the intention to bring about change that serves God and serves one another. Then we may justifiably hope that the change will indeed come.

1 Haman's promising day takes a turn

Esther 6

Esther's comedy is built upon reversals. Vashti is the one who was summoned by the king but did not come and was rejected for it; Esther is the one who came to the king without being summoned and was accepted despite it. Esther is a passive character who obeys Mordecai, until the exchange in chapter 4, after which Esther takes charge and Mordecai is the one who obeys her.

In chapter 6, the day starts so well for Haman, as he goes to see about scheduling an execution party to rid himself once and for all of that pesky Mordecai. However, the villain is about to be made the fool. Before long, the king's second-in-command is leading his arch-enemy, the man whose name is all but carved on Haman's gallows, about the streets of Susa, proclaiming his enemy's greatness to all who can hear, while the enemy sits robed, atop the horse—and not just any horse but a crown-wearing horse.

Not surprisingly, this incident brings about a radical turnabout in Haman's mood. The conclusion of chapter 5 finds Haman with head held high, buoyed by the advice of his wife and his companions (5:14). A very different Haman returns home at the end of chapter 6, a man 'mourning' and now 'with his head covered' (6:12). Haman's changed mood is equalled by the changed outlook of his previously supportive wife and companions. Those who formerly seemed certain of Haman's victory over Mordecai have shifted their position by 180 degrees. In a foretaste of what is to come on a grander scale, their confident advice, 'kill the Jew Mordecai', becomes a prediction of doom: 'that Jew Mordecai is going to get you' (6:13).

As the story progresses, the reversals will continue to build. Haman will be hanged on the very gallows he had built for Mordecai (7:10), while Mordecai is promoted into Haman's former position at court (8:2). Then, in the pivotal reversal of the story, the one for which Esther risked her life, the Jews will be transformed from the ones who would be destroyed, killed and annihilated (7:4) into those who will be permitted to destroy, to kill and to annihilate (8:11).

But for now, the chapter ends with Haman being whisked away to the banquet. While he may think his day can still be salvaged, those faintly ringing chimes of doom we were hearing earlier are now ringing more loudly. Today, Haman really should have stayed in bed.

2 Sometimes things just happen

Esther 7

Working alongside the hiddenness/surprise elements of humour, coincidence is another device of comedy that abounds in Esther. In Esther, things just happen. Mordecai just happens to be standing in the right place at the right time to overhear a plot to kill the king (2:21), which eventually leads to his advancement in power. Haman just happens to be in the court after the king is stricken with insomnia (6:4), after which Haman is forced to lead Mordecai around for his honour parade. In today's passage, coincidences make Haman's ever-worsening day plummet even further. The king just happens to reenter the room at the exact moment when Haman has flung himself on to Esther's bed to beg for mercy (v. 8), from which the king draws a rather incorrect, but not unsurprising, conclusion. Harbona, the eunuch, just happens to pop into court to remind the king of the gallows Haman has built (7:9), which are intended for Mordecai but in the end serve another purpose instead.

In a book in which God is never mentioned, some people find God's presence in these remarkable coincidences, as an unseen character working anonymously behind the scenes, a stage manager or director giving a helpful nudge or cue when the time is right. This is certainly one way to understand the unbelievable amount of 'happenstance' in the book of Esther.

As with hiddenness, however, comedy celebrates coincidence and embraces it without requiring any explanation for it. Unpredictable, sudden events bring both twists and resolutions, seemingly out of nowhere. These coincidences complicate the plot in ways that make the audience both shake their heads in disbelief and hold their sides in laughter.

3 More Jews today than yesterday

Esther 8

Wordplay is one of the most often used, but also most fragile, components of comedy. It is easily lost in the translation from one language to another, from one culture to another and from one time to another. Furthermore, wordplay is easily lost in explanation as well as translation. It is not surprising, then, that little, if any, wordplay from Hebrew makes it through the transition of language, culture or time, or through explanation, into modern English versions.

Despite this disclaimer, however, one of the best and, in my view, funniest wordplays of Old Testament Hebrew occurs at the end of chapter 8 and actually translates into English in a fairly understandable way. The strange word rendered by the NRSV as the phrase 'professed to be Jews' (v. 17) is found nowhere else in the Old Testament, and debate as to its meaning is ongoing. The phrase, more literally translated, would be something like 'made themselves Jews'. The meaning remains unclear, but, in light of this new irreversible edict (which reverses the previous irreversible edict), many people probably thought that the prudent move would be to get themselves a spot on the winning side—to do what needed to be done to ensure they were standing alongside, rather than in front of, the killing, destroying, annihilating machine when it storms on to the pitch. Finally, the Jews are at the top of the heap, and foreigners are trying to be like them!

Previously we discussed the creation of boundaries in humour. As long as we identify with the ones telling the joke, it is likely that we will get the joke and the joke will be found funny. How different the view looks, however, from the other side. It was Haman who celebrated the first edict and Mordecai who was weepin' and wailin'. Now Haman is hanging dead more than 22 metres up, and all the Jews—along with all the new Jewish converts—are the ones down at the pub.

4 Fewer Persians today than yesterday

Esther 9:1–19

As mentioned in the introduction, the violence of this passage is discomfiting and can turn smiles into furrowed brows. Interpreters have variously ignored, explained away or exegetically danced around this part of Esther. Even the Lectionary succumbs. On Esther's only lectionary Sunday, the verses given are 7:1–10 and 9:20–22, neatly excising today's reading.

Yet, keeping our eyes for comedy focused on the text will deliver us from our interpretive predicament. How? Because violence always has its place in comedy. Comedy frequently utilises, and sometimes even requires, aggression and hostility for its purposes. Violence in comedy offers not a model to be enacted, but rather an opportunity for escape and for catharsis, a release for pent-up aggression and hostility.

Imagine a tense room in which even the weakest joke is welcomed with vigorous laughter as people feel relief at having escaped the stress, even if only for a moment. Imagine, then, how much worse it must have been for the Israelites, living under the thumb of yet another foreign rule. And so the story of Esther is born: the worse they feel, the bigger the story gets; the harder they laugh, the better they feel. Catharsis and escape, like boundary-drawing, are important functions of comedy.

An important distinction exists between the violence of Esther and the violence in our world: Esther's violence is story-violence. The killing in Esther is not any more 'real' than a 187-day drinking party, or the depletion of a kingdom's marriageable young women, or a gallows built taller than any ladder that could reach its top. As in an episode of *Road Runner and Coyote*, we can live vicariously through the story-violence, speeding away, all smiles, as the anvil smashes our enemy into the shape of a walking accordion.

That's the gift comedy gives us. We can escape for a time to an unreal place; we are free to roam the side streets of our imagination, acting out fantasies of 'what if…' and relieving what has been stuffed down inside us. But after all this imagining and guffawing and throwing and dodging of anvils, the story ends and we know that it is just a story, and a rather funny one at that. Esther cannot be comedy for eight chapters, then something else for the final two. Reading Esther through the eyes of comedy holds it together as a story in which the Jews can imagine they wield power over the life and death of their enemies, having wrested it slyly from the dupes who govern them. Comedy offers a release and an escape, and the writers of Esther take advantage of that offer.

5 Purim begins

Esther 9:20–28

Ultimately, Esther is a story about survival, and it has a distinct message regarding how to guarantee this survival: work from within the system and maintain it, while finding a proper place within it. Offer no direct resistance, because it does not work. This does not, however, preclude us from finding the system ludicrous, ridiculous, stupid. Esther is the contrast to Vashti, who is eliminated when she threatens the establishment, refusing to conform to its demands. Esther herself, in approaching the king uninvited and devising a scheme to expose Haman, does exhibit a spirit of boldness and subversiveness. However, the book itself sends a more cautious and conservative overall message, discouraging open rebellion and encouraging a more institutionalised method of power acquisition.

For the Israelite people, exile was a shocking humiliation; so, for these people in diaspora, fantasising about paying back the powers-that-be was a predictable course for their thoughts and their stories to take. So the door opens for comedy to enter. For Jews living in diaspora, the humour of Esther offers an outlet for dreams and fantasies, for aggression and hostility. Unable physically to overthrow the powers established over them, they can utilise comedy to overthrow them in another way. Through Esther, the Jews can maintain their own sense of identity by making the Persians a ridiculed 'other'. They can subvert the establishment and prevail over it. The added bonus is that using this form of attack poses no danger to their bodily survival, because their assault is indirect and their subversion is contained in a story world. In the story, they risk themselves to prevail, while, in actuality, they have only taken the risk that someone might take offence at their story.

Using this vicarious tool, not only do the Israelites live another day to tell another story, they also survive through the annual celebration of Purim, a word derived from 'the lot' that Haman threw to choose the day of destruction (3:7). In this carnival-like celebration, year after year, the Jews once again experience a glorious victory over their oppressors, once again turning the tables on those who would seek to kill, destroy and annihilate them, as well as on those who are foolish enough to think they have the upper hand over God's chosen people.

6 Happily ever after

Esther 9:29—10:3

Comedy, in most or all of its guises, can be a deeply subversive force. Irony, satire, sarcasm, hyperbole—all have within their range the ability to undermine power. At its subversive best, humour destabilises the status quo, disrupts the established order and threatens the established power. As the achievements of Esther and Mordecai are recorded in today's passage, we see the subversiveness of comedy at work: an orphan and a man who spent his days lurking around the king's gate, two Jews living under the rule of a foreign power... become a queen and the king's second-in-command. They are portrayed as powerful leaders in their realm and among their people, as their achievements become part of the recorded history of not one but two peoples. Comedy loves underdogs, and this pair are the unlikeliest of heroes who subvert from within, comically undermining the structures and institutions of the society in which they are forced to live.

The powerful are dethroned, the powerless triumphant. Top dogs fall and underdogs rise. This is the nature of comedy—a world turned downside-up as expectation is surprised and as what ought to be finally becomes what is. This, too, is the nature of the gospel. As we enter the season of Advent, we commence our season of expectant waiting for the one who came and the one who is to come. His coming is filled with expectation, but his coming will defy our expectation, upending it, inverting it, transforming it. This is the subversive comedy of the nativity. The Christ child? The Christ child. Surely, you jest.

And so we come to the end of our story, a story that will be told again and again as, each year, an unexpected and extraordinary victory is celebrated. This is a story that promises to end well for everyone.

Except Haman. And his ten sons. And the 75,800 people who were violently slaughtered. But everyone else... lives happily ever after!

Guidelines

Being on the lookout for humour is a fresh but also instructive way to read and interpret the Bible. This approach, undertaken through the eyes of faith, takes us even further, though—far beyond just what is funny and through a door to a whole different way of seeing the world. When wielded well, comedy's ability to subvert is probably its most powerful weapon; and, in the world opened up by the Bible's humour, comedy's subversiveness has done its work and done it well. This is a world turned downside-up, where the last are first, where the unbelievable happens as a matter of course, where there are no losers because there are no underdogs, where there are no victims because there are no oppressors, where those who willingly sacrifice themselves are the ones who hold real and lasting power.

Esther says to all would-be oppressors, 'You have no power over us, because in our reality you are a ridiculous laughing stock, and you will not prevail.' And while God is not mentioned at all in the book of Esther, I believe that this attitude of the Jews is born out of their hope in a God who has promised never to let the oppressors have the final say. It is the same hope that we, as Christians, have in a God who would not even let the finality of death prevail.

As the diaspora Jews lived in their world, we live in this one, but we are also given chances to experience a reality that transcends this one, a world in which the meek are strong, in which tragedy never trumps hope, in which a man three days in the grave rises to live again. So we can stand with the Jews in Persia and laugh in the face of all this world can toss our way. This laughter will redeem us: it will save us from a world determined to revere power and wealth and violence and self-centredness, and deliver us to a life of communion and peace in God through Christ—a place we might call the kingdom of God.

FURTHER READING

Timothy K. Beal, *Esther* (Berit Olam series) (Liturgical Press, 1999).

Peter L. Berger, *Redeeming Laughter: The Comic Dimension of Human Experience* (Walter de Gruyter, 1997).

Adele Berlin, *Esther: The Traditional Hebrew Text With the New JPS Translation* (JPS Bible Commentary) (Jewish Publication Society, 2001).

Athalya Brenner (ed.), 'Are We Amused?: Humour About Women in the Biblical Worlds', *Journal for the Study of the Old Testament Supplement* 383 (T&T Clark International, 2003).

Athalya Brenner and Yehuda T. Radday (eds.), 'On Humour and the Comic in the Hebrew Bible', Bible and Literature Series, 23; *Journal for the Study of the Old Testament Supplement* 92 (Almond, 1990).

Don't forget to renew your annual subscription to *Guidelines*!
If you enjoy the notes, why not also consider giving a gift subscription to a friend or member of your family?

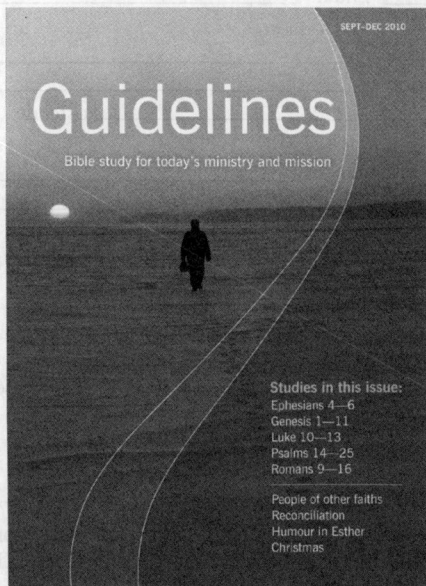

SEPT–DEC 2010

Guidelines

Bible study for today's ministry and mission

Studies in this issue:
Ephesians 4—6
Genesis 1—11
Luke 10—13
Psalms 14—25
Romans 9—16

People of other faiths
Reconciliation
Humour in Esther
Christmas

You will find a subscription order form overleaf.
Guidelines is also available from your local
Christian bookshop.

SUBSCRIPTIONS

- ❏ Please send me a Bible reading resources pack
- ❏ I would like to take out a subscription myself (complete your name and address details only once)
- ❏ I would like to give a gift subscription (please complete both name and address sections below)

Your name _____

Your address _____

_____ Postcode _____

Tel _____ Email _____

Gift subscription name _____

Gift subscription address _____

_____ Postcode _____

Gift message (20 words max.) _____

Please send *Guidelines* beginning with the January 2011 issue:

(please tick box)	UK	SURFACE	AIR MAIL
GUIDELINES	❏ £14.40	❏ £15.90	❏ £19.20
GUIDELINES 3-year sub	❏ £36.00		
GUIDELINES pdf version	❏ £11.40 (UK and overseas)		
GUIDELINES printed + *New Daylight* by email	❏ £23.40	❏ £24.90	❏ £28.20

Confirm your email address _____

Please complete the payment details below and send, with appropriate payment, to: **BRF, 15 The Chambers, Vineyard, Abingdon OX14 3FE.**

Total enclosed £ _____ (cheques should be made payable to 'BRF')

Please charge my Visa ❏ Mastercard ❏ Switch card ❏ with £ _____

Card number ▢▢▢▢▢▢▢▢▢▢▢▢▢▢▢▢▢▢▢▢

Expires ▢▢▢▢ Security code ▢▢▢ Issue no (Switch only) ▢▢▢▢

Signature (essential if paying by credit/Switch) _____

BRF is a Registered Charity

Romans 9—16

If biblical scholars have debated the meaning of much in Romans, this is particularly the case for Romans 9—11, where almost everything is controversial. But perhaps some of the debate can be sidestepped by attempting at every point to understand how these three chapters fit into both what has gone before in Romans 1—8 and what follows in Romans 12—16. As shall be seen, in Romans 12—16 the matter of the relationship between Jew and Gentile is further developed, on the basis of Paul's argument in Romans 9—11. And what about the significance of Romans 1—8? Having spoken about how God's covenant faithfulness has been fulfilled in Christ (Romans 1—4), and detailed how this fulfilment looks when arranged against the backdrop of the Jewish story of slavery, redemption and inheritance (Romans 5—8), Paul naturally turns to ask a question which has been in the background all along: if God's promises are fulfilled at last, what about ethnic Israel?

These notes are based on the New Revised Standard Version.

1 The difficult question

Romans 9:1–5

The introduction above highlights the question pressing on Paul in light of his claim that God's covenant faithfulness has been revealed in Christ: given an unbelieving Israel, how is God's faithfulness evident? In 9:1–5, Paul expresses the depth and nature of the problem involved, the matter to be addressed in the choppy waters of Romans 9—11.

The tragedy for Paul of unbelieving Israel, though not directly stated, is clear immediately; it is the cause of his 'unceasing anguish' (v. 2). So the questions he will now address are far from merely academic. Like Moses, he stands before God offering himself on Israel's behalf: 'But now, if you will only forgive their sin—but if not, blot me out of the book that you have written' (Exodus 32:32). Why have the Israelites turned from what God has done in Jesus? After all, ethnic Israel enjoys a number of covenant privileges: 'the adoption, the glory, the covenants, the giving of the law, the worship… the promises [and] the patriarchs' (vv. 4–5). In the Pentateuch, God's election and deliverance of Israel from Egypt occasionally employed adoption (or at least familial) metaphors (Exodus 4:22–23; Deuteronomy 14:1–2). The mention of 'glory' likewise conjures Old Testament depictions of the 'manifest presence of God'. The reference to 'covenants' probably indicates the several covenants mentioned in the Old Testament narratives, such as God's covenants with Noah, Abraham, Moses, David and so on. Given that Paul speaks of the patriarchs immediately after mention of 'the promises', it is likely that the Abrahamic promises are in his mind, as well as the way those promises found further development and expression in the prophetic writings.

Although Israel enjoys all these privileges, they have largely rejected the Messiah. So most terrible of all is that the Messiah indeed came from their bloodline. The best way of translating verse 5 remains disputed, but it could be that Paul is calling Christ 'God'. So the NIV reads, 'From them is traced the human ancestry of Christ, who is God over all.' If this is correct, could Paul be hinting at the vast extent of the tragedy involved in Israel's rejection of this Messiah?

It is noteworthy that Paul has spoken of those 'in Christ' in terms of just these privileges (God's adoption of *Christians*, of the fulfilment *in Christ* of the covenant, the promises to the patriarchs, and so on). In other words, the spiritual blessings of Gentile believers in Rome do not supersede but share in these Israelite blessings. If that is so, perhaps a background plea can already be heard: these Gentile believers should now share Paul's concern that so many Israelites have tragically rejected their Messiah. As is to be expected, though, a far deeper and theological problem lurks under these concerns, which we will see clearly in the next section.

2 From Abraham to the exodus

Romans 9:6–18

If ethnic Israel has rejected its Messiah and thus the fulfilment of God's promises and their covenant privileges listed in the previous verses, has God really been faithful to his covenant? If the descendants of those to whom he made promises, the Israelites, do not experience the fulfilment of the promises in Christ, does this not suggest that God's righteousness was actually not demonstrated in the faithfulness of Jesus? Unbelieving Israel is a massive theological problem for Paul, one that he must at last confront. Paul addresses these thorny questions by retelling the story of Israel, from Abraham to Paul's present day (Romans 9:6—10:21). This is quite typical of the earliest Jewish Christians: remember how Stephen, in Acts 7, told the story of Israel in his speech at his trial before the Sanhedrin. In Paul's narration he is (again) at pains to show how God has indeed been faithful to his covenant, and how this faithfulness reaches its expression in Christ.

His first response does not water down his commitment to the revelation of God's covenant faithfulness in Christ: it is certainly not 'as though the word of God had failed' (v. 6). God has not been unfaithful, because not all ethnic Israel are truly Israel—that is, those to whom the promises were made. Remember the covenant family: Abraham—Isaac—Jacob/Israel. God's promises to Abraham came only through Isaac, not his other son Ishmael. Then again, the promise came through Isaac's son Jacob, not Esau, Isaac's firstborn.

Having spoken in terms of the original patriarchs (vv. 6–13), Paul now speaks in light of the exodus (vv. 14–18). The question in verse 14 ('Is there injustice/unrighteousness on God's part?') reflects the sort of questions Paul asked earlier in Romans (for example, 3:5), and it reflects the key question now being addressed, namely Israel's unfaithfulness and the challenge therein to God's righteousness. The question is thus to be understood in light of the story of Israel, and is not best understood if it is detached from these moorings. So, when he raises the question about God's supposed 'injustice' (v. 14) and then refutes the claim with emphasis on his sovereignty, Paul is not encouraging speculation about the nature or purpose of God's election of individuals to salvation. Rather, he is speaking about the history of the patriarchs and the exodus, to answer the question implicitly set at the beginning of this chapter: is God faithful in the light of Israelite unbelief? An answer emerges: God has not been unfaithful: look at the founding story of Israel.

3 From the exodus to exile

Paul has not finished following the story of Israel, and he will do much with it yet. Having begun with the patriarchs and moved on to the exodus, Paul now speaks in terms of the exile. At this point in Israel's story, God judges his chosen people and few are left, just a small remnant. The exile motif is echoed in Paul's choice of pottery language, a famous image from the book of Jeremiah, which spoke of God's judgment of idolatrous Israel yet God's future restoration of his people on the other side of judgment, involving a new covenant (see Jeremiah 18; 31:31–34; also Isaiah 29 and 45). Simply put, the image of the potter affirms God's faithfulness to his promises, in and through the experience of exile, despite the fact that the majority of Israel had rebelled and rejected God's word.

The section is completed with four biblical quotations, two from Hosea and two from Isaiah. The passages in Hosea (1:10; 2:23) speak of God's faithfulness to his promises on the other side of judgment. However, Paul makes Hosea elaborate a point already touched on: God is able to remould the people of God as he chooses for the benefit of the world as a whole. The 'return from exile' people are those 'whom he has called, not from the Jews only but also from the Gentiles' (v. 24).

The passage in verses 27–28 comes from Isaiah 10:22–23, which explicitly refers to the original promise to Abraham ('the number of the children of Israel were like the sand of the sea'). Paul here argues that God's faithfulness to this promise is not jeopardised by the fact that only a remnant will be saved. God must be righteous not just in the sense that he is faithful but also in the sense that he judges sin, but, because he is righteous also in the sense that he is faithful, a remnant will be saved. Israel will not be obliterated like Sodom and Gomorrah (v. 29; Isaiah 1:9).

When reading passages like 9:22–23, it is important to remember that Paul is not detailing an abstract theology, merely decorating that construct with Bible verses as he sees fit. Rather, Paul's treatment of his scriptural passages reflects a theological rereading of the significance of Israel's story with God, in terms of the problem posed to God's covenant faithfulness by an Israel that has largely rejected its Messiah. Once these coordinates are kept in mind, some modern theological debates can be circumvented.

4 From exile to God's covenant faithfulness in Christ

Romans 9:30—10:21

A major reason why Paul has addressed his questions through a retelling of the story of Israel now becomes clear. Having gone from the patriarchs to the exodus and the exile, Paul now moves to the Messiah. This way of reading the unfinished story of the Old Testament as reaching its climax in Christ was a typical early Christian approach to theology (see, for example, the genealogy in Matthew 1; the use of scriptural prophecy in Luke 1—2).

To be remembered once again is the prophetic pattern: with the restoration of the twelve tribes from exile (and associated themes such as the making of the new covenant, the gift of the Spirit and so on), the Gentiles would at last be blessed according to the Abrahamic covenant (see Genesis 12:3): Exile –> Restoration –> Blessings to nations.

Because God has indeed been faithful to his covenant, despite large-scale Israelite rejection of the Messiah, Paul can now explain how the gospel of Jesus addresses all nations and peoples. Again, this release of blessings to Gentiles comes about because Christ, as Israel's representative, was faithful to the covenant. God could at last bring blessing to a world under the power of sin, could at last reveal his righteousness, through the faithfulness of Christ for all who believe. The 'righteousness that is based on the law' did not get ethnic Israel far, but rather landed them in exile awaiting redemption (9:30–33). So Paul's prayer is that Israel may be saved because there is redemption in Christ Jesus, who has at last brought the story of Israel, and Torah, to its goal/end (10:4).

In 10:5–13, Paul explains how this salvation comes to all, both Jew and Gentile—that is, through the faith-confession that Jesus is Lord, through entering into the realm of the risen Lordship of Jesus Christ. Indeed, Paul's use of scriptural echoes and citations in this passage (see the use of Deuteronomy 30:12–14 in 10:6–8) highlights once again that through Jesus Christ the covenant is fulfilled, and through faith in him the blessings of the covenant are enjoyed.

Romans 10:14–21 does not add further to the story of the patriarchs, the exodus, the exile and the goal found in Christ, but rather draws out a few points that are already or shortly will be established. The good news of the return from exile, as declared in Isaiah 52:7 and cited by Paul in verse

15, is found in 'the word of Christ' (v. 17). Israel's prophetically foreseen rejection of this word will be countered by the strategy of making Israel jealous by the Gentile reception of their own covenant blessings.

5 A remnant

Romans 11:1–10

This treatment of Israel's story, from the patriarchs, through the exodus and the exile, climaxing in the Messiah, leads inevitably and pointedly to the questions asked in Romans 11, which focus on the future of ethnic Israel in God's redemptive purposes. More immediately, though, the previous reiteration of the basic problem of Israelite unbelief leads Paul to a more sustained consideration of the nature of the Jewish rejection of Jesus: has God rejected his people (v. 1)?

Just as the promise of restoration is promised for all in Christ precisely as the fulfilment of God's story with Israel, so Paul explains that despite widespread rejection of salvation in Christ, there is a remnant—and Paul himself belongs to it. God has not replaced Jews with Gentiles in his saving plans; he has emphatically not rejected his people, because God has saved a remnant, as in the exilic period (note here the reference to Elijah and the 'seven thousand who have not bowed the knee to Baal', 1 Kings 19:18). And this remnant exists not through careful law-observance, for failure to keep the law led to exile in the first place. Membership in the redeemed remnant comes only through the grace displayed in Christ.

This point needs to be remembered when Paul speaks shortly of the salvation of 'all Israel' (11:26). It is highly unlikely that Paul thought of a way of salvation for Israel apart from faith in Jesus Christ. His place in the remnant happened through the grace apart from law found through faith in Jesus Christ (see 3:21–22; 10:8–13).

In verses 7–10, Paul again cites a number of texts, not to make a new point but to reiterate what the elect have obtained, and what Israel has failed to receive. But what was Israel seeking? Israel was seeking the prophetically promised redemption, but tragically the people failed to recognise that this redemption was revealed in Christ. God was faithful to his covenant through the faithfulness of Jesus. Indeed, these same pro-

6–12 December

phetic texts had foretold that Israel would be hardened (see Paul's usage of Deuteronomy 29:4; Isaiah 29:10; Psalm 69:22–23). Once again, we need to be careful not to transport these texts into contemporary discussions about double-predestination and such like (that is, that God has elected not only some individuals for salvation but also some for damnation). Paul is drawing on a Jewish understanding of hardening which was what happened when God delayed judgment. Those who did not use this time to repent were hardened so that judgment, when it came, would be seen as entirely just.

6 In this way all Israel will be saved

Romans 11:11–36

Many people consider this passage to be one of the most majestic and important in Paul's letters, yet it is clouded by debated interpretations. Did Paul think that all Jews across time would be saved, or, rather, only those Jews living at the end? Or is Paul redefining 'Jew', as he has done in other parts of Romans (for example, 2:28–29), to mean that all Christians, both Jew and Gentile, will be saved? Scholars continue to dispute these and other questions. It is, at least, fairly uncontroversial to divide the text into four obvious sections: (a) vv. 11–16, (b) vv. 17–24, (c) vv. 25–32 and (d) vv. 33–36.

Just as Paul answers the question in 11:1 in the negative, so he offers a resounding 'no' to the question in verse 11 as to whether Israel has stumbled beyond hope. Indeed, Israel's story, as detailed in Romans 9—10, in a mysterious way prefigures the story of Christ. Just as Christ suffered rejection and death, so Israel has experienced suffering in judgment, cast off from God. But just as Christ has been raised from the dead, bringing salvation to all, so too the 'acceptance' of Israel will mean resurrection!

Indeed, Israel has not been cast off for ever, but Gentiles are only grafted into the covenant blessings that are originally Israel's. What is more, if Israel begins to believe in the revelation of the righteousness of God in Jesus the Messiah, they will themselves be grafted back in. In light of this, Paul can also draw the pastoral–theological judgment that Gentiles, too, must be aware of both the kindness and severity of God. They will be treated no differently from Israel. The Gentiles are not privileged above the Jews, any more than the Jews are over the Gentiles.

Verses 25–32 are a high point. The hardening of Israel and the consequent salvation of Gentiles is the way in which 'all Israel will be saved'. The wider context of Romans suggests that 'Israel' is meant here to indicate believing Jews and Gentiles (see 9:6). The immediate context, however, suggests otherwise (see 11:25, where 'Israel' means ethnic Israel). Paul could mean to indicate all the elect of Israel, but the matter remains disputed. Either way, Paul probably does not mean to refer to a distant future salvation of all Israel. Paul's citation and subtle alteration of Isaiah 59:20–21 suggests that the salvation of all Israel is now, at last, happening through Christ the Deliverer. Indeed, following the pattern of death and resurrection both in Israel and in Christ, Paul finishes his argument with the astonishing assertion that 'God has imprisoned all in disobedience so that he may be merciful to all' (v. 32). All! This conclusion shows why Paul answered the implicit question in 9:1–5 via a retelling of the story of Israel. From election to death and exile and finally to restoration, the people of Israel have in mysterious respects embodied the story of their Messiah in his life, death and resurrection. Appropriately, this all leads Paul to a statement of praise (vv. 33–36).

Guidelines

In Romans 9—11, Paul wrestled with perhaps the most difficult problem confronting his confidence that Christ's faithfulness is the revelation of the long-awaited covenant faithfulness of God. The very fact that he spent three long, detailed chapters on the matter is a lesson in itself. Do we also honestly confront the difficult questions raised by our theology, by our preaching and teaching, by the issues raised in our pastoral efforts? Or do we often simply avoid the 'elephant in the room'? How might we learn from Paul's bold and honest approach?

As a Jew, Paul's natural heart's desire was that Israel might be saved. Are our desires also formed out of godly concern for the salvation of others? How can we cultivate the expression of godly desire in our prayers?

Paul's detailed theological reasoning in Romans 9—11 leads him to astonished worship. How can our theology and Bible study best lead us to worship?

1 Ethical living in a new age

Romans 12

On the basis of all that has been said, Paul can now turn to several practical matters, mixing general advice with more specifically focused counsel (chs. 12—13 are more general, laying the foundation for the more specific injunctions in chs. 14—15). Hence 12:1 reads, 'I appeal to you therefore, brothers and sisters'. It is crucial to remember that a sharp division between matters 'ethical' and 'theological' would have made little sense to Paul. After all, Romans 6 and 8, the heartland of Paul's 'theological' reasoning, contains much that is 'ethical'. It is rather typical that Paul's ethics is theological and his theology is ethical. That said, there is a clear distinction in style and content, in Romans 12—16, from what has preceded it.

Straight away, care must be taken not to understand Paul's teaching here as simply implying that Christians, by the power of the Spirit, can live a bit more ethically than others. Rather, Paul frames Romans 12 and 13 with the sort of language that speaks of 'ages' and 'world orders'. So Paul writes, 'Do not be conformed to this world/age' (12:2). A new age has begun, and Christians are to live as is appropriate in that new age. It is about living in a different age, not simply ethical improvement.

If we remember Romans 8, by 'spiritual' worship Paul can hardly mean 'non-physical' worship. Indeed, the Greek word suggests that the worship is 'logical' or 'reasonable', so presenting our bodies in worship is the 'logical' thing to do. In doing this, the Christian has a renewed mind to discern God's will: ethical living, for Paul, is certainly not just about lists of 'dos and don'ts'.

The instructions in Romans 12 are fairly generally applicable (and notice how they tend to focus on sustaining healthy communal relationships), yet one or two may cause surprise. First, what does 'prophecy, in proportion to faith' mean (v. 6)? It probably means that the prophet should only speak in ways consistent with the faith of the church. Second, some of the material in verses 14–21 may sound strange. Do 'leaving room for the wrath of God' and 'heaping burning coals on their heads' sound like loving motivations, the sort that Paul indeed urged in the previous verses (vv. 9–13)? Paul is a realist (as verse 18 clearly shows!) and he simply provides reason for Christians not to take vengeance into their own hands. In 'heaping coals', Paul shows a process that could indeed lead to the offender's repentance through experiencing the burning guilt of godly remorse.

Finally, the instructions in verses 14–21 are probably to be read in terms of the relationships that Christians have with those outside the community of faith, a point that will potentially change how we read the text.

2 Love is the fulfilment of the law

Romans 13

'Let every person be subject to the governing authorities' (v. 1). 'Whoever resists authority resists what God has appointed' (v. 2). 'The authority does not bear the sword in vain' (v. 4). 'Pay taxes' and so on (v. 7).

These are some of the most controversial words in Paul's letters. Indeed, in light of the fact that Romans 13:1–7 was used by German Christians to justify support of the Third Reich, some modern New Testament scholars have argued that Paul might have wished he had never penned these words, given the way they have been (ab)used in church history.

Perhaps some of the difficulties of this passage can be managed by remembering three things. First, Paul was not writing a systematic and definitive statement of 'church and state', as if he would not indeed offer qualification to these statements, if pressed. He was writing a letter, with certain rhetorical goals to achieve, and this can sometimes lead to propositions that, from a systematic perspective, lack nuance. Second, the Jews had been expelled from Rome a few years before Paul's letter, due to what the Roman historian Suetonius described as constant disturbances 'at the instigation of Chrestus' (the name is possibly a corruption of 'Christ'). In other words, Christians had probably caused problems in the recent past, and Paul's rhetoric is directed to that situation. Third, the previous point hints at what the language of verses 1–7 makes clear: what Paul is opposed to is violent resistance, a point that is evident in the Greek connotations of the words used for 'resist'. So Paul does not exclude the kind of (also politically) subversive acts of love that he has already urged in this context ('overcome evil with good', 12:21). Roman emperors were called 'lord', 'son of God' and 'saviour', and their 'gospel' promised 'peace' and 'salvation' for all under their rule. So we cannot help but be impressed by Paul's political boldness when we read, for example, Romans 1:1–7.

Verses 8–10 drive the point home: love, not violence, is the fulfilment of the law: 'love does no wrong to a neighbour', as he puts it. This is not meant to mean that 'love is the way to earn righteousness through Torah', but rather that this is the way the renewed people of God are finally a blessing to the nations, as God promised to Abraham and as Paul expounded in Romans 4.

Verses 11–14 round off Romans 12—13 as the section started, by speaking again of a new age. Paul's instructions here are all about 'what time it is'. The night of the previous age is far gone; the dawn of the new is near.

3 The 'weak' and the 'strong'

Romans 14

We need to recall that Romans was probably written into a context of tension between Jewish and Gentile Christians. Indeed, it is likely that some Gentile Christians felt superior to Jewish believers, people who had probably only recently returned to the Roman church after a temporary exile from Rome because of an edict by Emperor Claudius (remember the comment of Suetonius mentioned above). The division between Jew and Gentile has been one of Paul's concerns throughout Romans. He has consistently urged that neither Jew nor Gentile is privileged in terms of salvation. All are sinners, and all are saved by grace through faith.

In Romans 14, Paul speaks again to two groups, the 'weak' and the 'strong', and, though some aspects of the 'faith' of the 'weak' seem to correspond with Jewish sensibilities (see vv. 2, 5), we should not draw the distinction between these groups according to ethnicity. For example, Paul himself was a Jewish Christian, and he certainly considered himself one of the 'strong'. Besides, by explicitly dividing the two groups according to their ethnicity, Paul would effectively shoot himself in the foot, emphasising what he has been at pains to refute—namely a supposed clear border line between Jew and Gentile. It is perhaps partly for this reason that the groups are left unnamed, and only in 15:7–13 does Paul speak of 'Gentiles' and 'the circumcision' (that is, Jews).

Paul's strategy in Romans 14 is pragmatic. Yes, there remain different opinions and convictions within legitimate expressions of Christian faith; so, differences accepted, we must learn to avoid judging or despising one another. This is the key point: we do not judge, for only the Master judges his servants (v. 4). In emphasising the Lordship of Christ as part of this argument, Paul shows the uniting factor for the Christians, much as he did in 12:5 ('we, who are many, are one body in Christ'). Just as YHWH is one, so every knee shall bow to the one risen Lord (see v. 11). The one Lord makes one people (see also 1 Corinthians 8; Ephesians 4:5).

Apparently, the matter of tensions between different groups in Rome was central to Paul's purpose in writing to them. So with this response outlined, Paul turns (vv. 13–23) to explore what this unity might look like in practice. Here, he ventures his own opinion on matters, framed with the appropriate attitude of humility, and urges for the primacy of love in one's actions. In 1 Corinthians 8—10, in a similar context involving 'weak' believers, Paul constructs a similar argument, urging the kind of self-sacrificial love that 'makes for peace and for mutual edification', as he puts it in Romans 14:19.

4 Jew and Gentile united in Christ

Romans 15:1–13

In many ways, 15:1–13 continues the argument from Romans 14. However, in other ways this section, especially verses 7–13, functions as the summary of the entire letter—a point that will be explained below.

The passage can be divided into two: verses 1–6 and 7–13. In the first part, Paul develops the point made in the previous chapter, summarising it in two commands: 'bear with the frailty of the weak' (a better translation than NRSV's 'put up with the failings') and 'please your neighbour'. Paul's principle is formulated negatively here: don't please yourself, because Christ didn't please himself. After citing scripture (which was 'written for our instruction', v. 4), Paul appeals for prayer for harmony so that God may be praised. In other words, there is a structure: (1) a command relating to the previous chapter; (2) a statement about the work of Christ; (3)

a scriptural citation; (4) a declaration about the goal—the praise of God.

This pattern is broadly repeated in verses 7–13. Verse 7 is another command following on from the previous chapter. There is a note on the significance of Jesus (v. 8), then scriptural citations (vv. 9–10) and a final note of praise (v. 11). Thus, both halves of 15:1–13 approach the matter from different angles, summarising the exhortations to unity (Romans 12—14) and grounding them in a Christ-centred reading of scripture (Romans 1—12).

But while verse 3 was formulated negatively, verse 8 is stated positively and ties in to the theme of the whole of Romans, bringing Paul's theological journey, throughout the letter, to a brief, crisp point: 'Christ has become a servant of the circumcised on behalf of the truth of God in order that he might confirm the promises given to the patriarchs, and in order that the Gentiles might glorify God for his mercy' (vv. 8–9). Christ has been faithful to God's covenant, as Israel's representative, and thus God's righteousness is now manifest—God's covenant faithfulness that would lead to the blessing of the nations, as originally promised to Abraham.

The background narrative runs as follows: Abrahamic covenant to bless world (undo the damage done in Genesis 3 to 11) →Exile →Restoration (because God is faithful to his promises to bless the world through his covenant) →Blessing to the nations (see, for example, Zechariah 8:8, 13). For Paul, Christ climaxes this story and initiates its eschatological fulfilment. Echoing language found throughout Romans 1, 3—4 and 9—11, Christ serves the circumcised with his faithfulness (ch. 3) and thereby confirms the promises to the patriarchs (chs. 4 and 9), so that the Gentiles might join in glorifying God for his mercy. This is the narrative logic that stands behind Paul's commands for unity between Jew and Gentile. Now united in the wake of God's faithfulness in Christ, they are recipients of God's saving blessing in accordance with the Abrahamic covenant. They are united in Christ for God's glory. The threads of Romans are here tied together.

5 Paul's travel plans

Romans 15:14–33

Modern formal letters tend to use established formats ('Dear Sir'/'Yours faithfully'). So did ancient Greek letters, in which a salutation (X greets Y) would be followed by a thanksgiving, then the body of the letter, then closing exhortations (often including travel plans) and finally a benediction. As an ancient Greek letter, Romans broadly follows this established format. The body of the letter has just ended (notice the tense of verse 15: 'I have written to you'), and now Paul enters his 'closing exhortations', which feature a detailed description of his travel plans.

In verses 14–24, Paul details his plans with a description of his missionary activities (vv. 14–21) and his explicit travel plans (vv. 23–24). In the first part, he speaks of Christ himself being present and active, by the Spirit, in and through his mission. So he boasts of what 'Christ has accomplished through' him 'by the power of the Spirit' (vv. 18–19). Interestingly, Paul seems to be thinking here of the risen Christ, in relation to the Spirit, in much the same way that Jews thought of God as present and active in and through the Spirit. In light of such data, it is little surprise that the Church later formulated a doctrine of Christ as being 'one substance with the Father' (Nicaea 325) and spoke of the triune identity of God.

Christ has been active in Paul's mission 'from Jerusalem and as far around as Illyricum' (the Balkan coast on the Adriatic Sea, facing Italy) (v. 19). This geographical information, coupled with the priestly vocabulary (see v. 16), suggests that Paul understood his own mission as, in some sense, the fulfilment of biblical prophecy, specifically Isaiah 66:18–21. But Paul will not stop at Illyricum. After visiting Jerusalem to deliver money for the poor, which had been collected throughout Macedonia and Achaia, he planned missionary work in Spain (v. 24), stopping off in Rome on the way. Of course, other parts of the New Testament tell us that Paul was then arrested in Jerusalem and sent to prison, so he had to wait a few years before his visit to Rome could take place—and, as the prayer request in verse 31 makes clear, Paul was aware of these potential dangers.

Missionary work in Spain would mark a new phase in his apostolic activities. There is no evidence of Jewish synagogues in Spain in the first century, which means that Paul would be setting foot on a land entirely unfamiliar with the scriptures, the notion of Messiah and so on. This was a bold venture, but Paul was driven by a passion to name Christ where he had not been named (see v. 20), to go where no one had gone before.

This section, as the format of ancient Greek letters would dictate, finishes with an explicit exhortation: here to 'earnest prayer' (vv. 30–32).

6 Greetings and exhortations

In finishing Romans 15 with the benediction 'The God of peace be with all of you. Amen', it would seem that Paul had actually finished his letter. Yet we have a Romans 16, containing commendation and greetings (vv. 1–16), exhortation to avoid dissension (vv. 17–20), greetings from colleagues (vv. 21–24) and a concluding doxology (a short statement of praise) (vv. 25–27). The various original Greek manuscripts of Romans often omit this last chapter, and some scholars argue that it is unlikely that Paul would have known so many people, as is evidenced in these verses, in a city he had never visited. So some think that chapter 16 was added to the end of Romans by later scribal editors. Paul wrote it, but perhaps it originally belonged elsewhere, as a cover letter for the courier as he or she passed through key locations on the journey to Rome. Furthermore, the final doxology, likewise, finds itself in various positions in the Greek manuscripts, so some think it was written later as a better conclusion to the original Romans, which may have lacked chapter 16. Either way, our canonical Romans now includes Romans 16, so to Romans 16 we shall go!

Having commended Phoebe, verses 3–15 give a long list of personal greetings. Much attention has been drawn to the female name of Junia in verse 7, whom Paul describes as 'prominent among the apostles'. The significance of this for modern church structures and gender roles is clear: one of the foundation apostles of Christianity was a woman.

Paul rounds off his greetings with an exhortation to 'greet one another with a holy kiss' (v. 16). While not a proof text for Christian speed-dating, the 'holy kiss' may have been a part of the earliest Christian worship practice. Ambrosiaster (the name given to an unknown late fourth-century Christian biblical exegete) adds that the kissing is not 'in carnal desire, but in the Holy Spirit'; the participants are 'devout, not carnal'!

Verses 17–20 include an exhortation to watch out for those who cause division. While this may have been applicable anywhere in Paul's churches, it does strike the important chord reverberating throughout Romans, namely the unity of the one people of God, Jew and Gentile, in Christ.

After the final greetings from Paul's colleagues (where a certain Tertius identifies himself as the letter writer—it was common in those days for a secretary to take a role in letter writing, whether as transcriber, contributor or even composer), the letter is ended with a glorious statement of praise. Whether Paul penned the words or not, they sum up very nicely the key themes in Romans: Jesus Christ is the revelation of the hidden mystery (of God's covenant faithfulness), made known through the prophetic writings (as Paul has repeated throughout), so that the Gentiles are blessed.

Guidelines

It was suggested above that Romans 14 is a pragmatic encouragement for Christian unity, one that nevertheless wholly accepts the presence of different expressions of faith within one community. There is unity in diversity. How might this approach speak into our relationships and church communities?

Having reached the end of this overview of Romans, it must immediately be noted that the reading proposed is only one of many. In academic circles, a similar variation has both its supporters and detractors. In other words, different ways of approaching and understanding the argument of this letter may ultimately prove more persuasive and true to the apostle. But rather than allowing such thoughts to undermine our efforts in grappling with Romans, perhaps this is a lesson in itself: despite our differences, let each of us strive to be fully convinced in our own minds, to offer our interpretations in honour of the Lord (see Romans 14:5–6), and to live worshipfully in ways that resonate with God's glorious gospel. As a result of your time in Romans, for what fresh insights and encouragements can you begin to praise God?

It is ironic that many Christians have broken away from other Christians on the basis of Romans, when Paul has attempted here to provide his fullest description of the way God has brought Christians together from diverse ethnic and theological backgrounds, to unite them in Christ. But perhaps we have something else to learn here. After Paul has said so much about the gospel, even he can only exclaim, 'How unsearchable are [God's] judgments and how inscrutable [God's] ways!' (11:33). Should we not also assume the position of theological and exegetical humility and, when all is said and done, simply 'stand in awe' (11:20) rather than presume to have solved every puzzle? In God's sovereignty, Romans teaches us one of the hardest yet most liberating lessons of all—worshipful humility.

Christmas

Waiting, receiving, living: these are the themes of the next two weeks. The biblical texts are mainly those set for this season by the Revised Common Lectionary (readings common to the Church of England, Roman Catholic, Methodist and United Reformed Churches), so we will be reflecting together with a great many Christians over this crucial fortnight in the Christian year. We listen with voices from the Old and New Testaments, readings with obvious connections with Advent and Christmas, and those that help us connect our thinking and praying with the whole Christian faith. The Bible was compiled by the Christian Church, so it is fitting that we read it in common with the Church too: we will gain additional strength from knowing that we are not praying and reflecting alone but that these passages and themes are ones that our fellow believers are subjecting to equally intense appreciation.

The scriptures at this hectic time of year actually bid us pause and calm ourselves, taking comfort from a God who is always already on his way towards us and who wants nothing more than to strengthen us in our witness as we abide in the body of his Son, Jesus Christ our Lord.

These notes are based on the New Revised Standard Version.

20–26 December

1 Bothering God

Isaiah 7:10–14

Rather splendidly in this busy last week of Advent, when we may find our patience frequently tried, it seems that God has a similar experience. The eighth-century BC monarch Ahaz is asked to perform a simple task, which should be rather congenial—to ask for a sign from God. Frequently we complain that God does not reveal himself, that discerning his will is very hard. When asked, 'How do we discern God's will?' the 20th-century Anglican monk Fr Gabriel Hebert responded laconically, 'We can't—that's the joke.' So it seems all the more odd that Ahaz should refuse to do this when asked. He even offers a pious reason for refusing (v. 12).

We too can have an excessively human view of God as one with limited patience and minimal interest in our lives, and sound almost pious in so doing. People will often say, 'Oh, I didn't like to bother God with that; it didn't seem important enough' or 'I've already asked for quite a lot'. Yet Isaiah reminds us that if anything tries God's patience, it's us imagining that he hasn't got much of it, treating him as if he were another human being, albeit a very big one. Eight centuries later, God himself will tell a joke on exactly that theme when, in the 18th chapter of Luke's Gospel, Jesus amusingly compares his Father to an irritable old judge who will give us what we want just to shut us up.

Yet Ahaz may have been right to be cautious, because the sign he is given by God is not only mysterious but far greater than he anticipated. The mystery entails who this son is: is it Hezekiah, the son of Ahaz; or a son for Isaiah; or the Messiah himself? It will take over 700 years to find out. Isaiah urges us, therefore, to be patient, not to become weary in our calls on and prayers to our mysterious God, but to be confident that he is never weary of us. Isaiah also urges us to be prepared for receiving (as the Anglican prayer for the Twelfth Sunday after Trinity puts it) 'more than either we desire or deserve'. Ahaz is worried that the combined forces of Aram and Ephraim will attack Jerusalem and defeat him, and is looking only for words of guidance and encouragement, yet what he gets is the promise of Emmanuel—'God with us'.

2 Desiring God

Song of Solomon 2:8–14

Desire can sometimes get a bad press. The Anglican Book of Common Prayer urges us to confess the 'devices and desires of our own hearts', and many a saint is venerated for having gained control over their 'passions'. The doctrine of God's impassibility (that he isn't changed by being acted upon from outside, and doesn't feel pleasure or pain as a result of what we do) can get mangled by people into suggesting some impersonal deity who doesn't care for us. Yet this text from the Song of Songs is one of many that put paid to such a notion. This text is nothing but desire, and gets into the Bible not just as a permanent witness to the goodness of human desire but also because it speaks of God's desire for his people. It is an excellent Advent reading, too, beginning, as so much in this season does, with a call to attention: 'The voice of my beloved! Look, he comes, leaping upon the mountains' (v. 8). An Advent hymn from the first centuries of Christianity urges the same: 'Hark! A herald voice is calling: Christ is nigh it seems to say' (trans. E. Caswell).

God is taking the initiative, coming bounding over the hills towards us. He does this not only because we cannot save ourselves and so need him to come to us, but because, as the early theologians taught, he is 'pure act'. The Holy Trinity is not an unchanging divine lump but an eternal relationship of love, the eternal pouring out of Father to Son and Son to Father, the pouring out of which is the Holy Spirit. God is never still but, utterly desiring us endlessly, comes towards us. This season of Advent is precisely the time each year when we are reminded that God is always coming towards us. At this time, we might imagine him coming rather as Christmas comes—a train hurtling unstoppably towards us and flattening everything in its path. Yet the Song of Solomon corrects this idea: he comes to coax and entice us as a lover does. He looks in through the lattice and speaks tenderly to us, inviting us to come to him. And, very beautifully, he says what he really thinks of us: 'Your voice is sweet, and your face is lovely' (v. 14).

3 Revolutionary God

Luke 1:46–56

In statues and paintings, the Blessed Virgin Mary is often portrayed with her head down-turned and hands together in prayer, an image of docility and receptiveness—the female equivalent of the 'Jesus, meek and mild' of Charles Wesley's 1742 hymn. Yet her song of praise, echoing Hannah's paean in thanksgiving for a son (1 Samuel 2:1–10), is one of a tough persistent disciple, who is set to endure the curious and maybe judgmental looks and comments of family and friends over the nine months of her remarkable pregnancy. Equally, Hannah was tormented by her husband's other wife for her inability to have children, seen at that time as a sign of failure and of God's disfavour. Yet she went to the temple and prayed fervently, promising that, if God granted her a son, he would be dedicated to the Lord. So Samuel, when he was born, was given to the priest Eli and lived away in the temple—surely an extraordinary sacrifice for a mother with (at that time) only one child, for whom she had waited for so long.

Mary, formed in the Hebrew scriptures, would have recognised much of this, and would have heard in her own experience the echo of her forerunner, Hannah. Perhaps she wondered if she too would be called to give up her son, though little imagining the extent of the sacrifice that both she and Jesus would later be expected to make.

Yet the God described in both Hannah's and Mary's songs is one who turns the world upside down—an action which, in a fallen world, will always involve sacrifice. 'He has brought down the powerful from their thrones, and lifted up the lowly; he has filled the hungry with good things, and sent the rich away empty,' Mary cries (vv. 52–53). She is the herald of justice, preparing the way for Jesus, just as John the Baptist will. She who is unmarried and of little account in the affairs of the world is to bear the Son of God. Her own body, therefore, is a sign of the revolutionary justice of God, and she proclaims that this is for everyone—all who fear him in every generation. The proud, powerful and rich will be scattered; the lowly, fearful and hungry will be welcomed in.

4 Dancing God

Luke 1:39–45

One of the big differences between going out dancing on a Friday night these days and, say, 100 years ago is that today you dance alone. The foxtrot or waltz require a partner, where you learn to move in step with one another. In the past, you couldn't dance on your own: dancing was, by definition, a social activity. These days, a tango on the nightclub dance floor (despite the best efforts of the BBC's *Strictly Come Dancing*) would look highly amiss. Each person dances alone, making their own moves, almost irrespective of their neighbour. It is a miniature of the individualism and atomisation of our society.

The encounter between these two loving cousins, Elizabeth and Mary, is one of old-fashioned dancing, or at least of genuine reciprocity. First Elizabeth sings, 'Blessed are you among women and blessed is the fruit of your womb' (v. 42) and then Mary sings her Magnificat (so called after the first word of the song in Latin). Elizabeth blesses Mary and Mary blesses God. There is even a piece of physical dancing—John leaping for joy in Elizabeth's womb. John dances a joyful jig in his mother's body, echoing the dance that King David performed before the ark of covenant in 2 Samuel 6:14–15. It is clearly recalling David's dance, because the Israelites believed that the ark, in holding the tablets of the law given to Moses, represented the presence of God. Now John the Baptist, on hearing Mary's voice, also dances before the ark—the ark of the new covenant. Mary's womb holds not the representation of the presence of God but the actual presence of God on earth, Jesus Christ. Confronted with that, who could refuse to dance?

So, if the pressure of the final days before Christmas is getting too much or words are not coming easily in prayer, then John the Baptist gives us fine biblical warrant for a little two-step. So find a partner and tread the light fantastic for the faith; although, if you do it during Holy Communion, expect some quizzical looks!

5 Naming God

Luke 1:67–79

Whenever I did something wrong at home, my name, usually foreshortened to 'Rob', would instantly be lengthened to 'Robert'. The use of my name told me exactly what mood my parents were in. In the Bible, names are incredibly important. Abram becomes Abraham, Jacob becomes Israel, Simon becomes Peter, and Saul becomes Paul—on each occasion, when God has something for them to do. A new name marks an important new stage in their lives.

It was not unreasonable for John the Baptist's family to expect him to have the family name—Zechariah, a good name for a prophet, one with precedent among the Old Testament books. Yet Zechariah's son is not to be just another prophet. He will prepare the way for a new covenant, a new blessing not only for Israel but for Gentiles too. Zechariah's offspring will point towards Jesus, the Son of God who is perfectly human and perfectly divine. So this child is given a new name as well—John—and John means

'The Lord gives grace'. In Jesus we are to receive the fullness of God: 'grace upon grace', as another John puts it in the prologue to his Gospel (1:16). How fitting, then, that the name of the Messiah (literally, Christos in Greek) should be Jesus, a Hebrew word meaning 'the Lord saves'. Not only does the name remind us once again of the initiative and priority of God—it is the Lord who saves, not us—but the first part of the Hebrew word for Jesus comes from God's mysterious name, given when Moses asks him who he is (Exodus 3:14). The Hebrew word YHWH was regarded as unspeakable by the Israelites, being a revelation too awesome to say. The closest translation is something along the lines of 'I am who I am'. If it tells us anything, it tells us that God is mysterious and there are no words by which we can capture him.

As we stand on the edge of Jesus' nativity, it is good to remember our baptism, our naming as disciples of Christ—when we, like John the Baptist, were given a vocation, a job to do. We are reminded that we, too, made in the image of God (Genesis 1:27), are a great and wonderful mystery.

6 The birth of God

Luke 2:1–7

Saint Augustine of Hippo (AD354–430) sums up the extraordinary miracle and paradox of this day:

He it is by whom all things were made, and who was made one of all things; who is the revealer of the Father, the creator of the Mother; the Son of God by the Father without a mother, the Son of man by the Mother without a father; the great day of the angels, little in the day of mortals; the Word who is God before all time, the Word made flesh at a fitting time; the maker of the sun, made under the sun; ordering all the ages from the bosom of the Father, hallowing a day of today from the womb of the Mother; remaining in the former, coming forth from the latter; author of the heaven and the earth, sprung under the heaven out of the earth; unutterably wise, in his wisdom a babe without utterance; filling the world, lying in a manger; ruling the stars, feeling for the breast with his infant lips; great in the form of God, tiny in the form of a servant, in such a way that neither was that greatness diminished by his tininess, nor was his tininess oppressed by that greatness. For when he took upon himself human members, he

did not abandon divine works, nor did he cease from reaching from end to end mightily and ordering all things sweetly. When having put on the weakness of the flesh he was received in the womb of the Virgin, he was not confined there, so that the good of wisdom was not withdrawn from the angels, and that we might taste and see how sweet the Lord is.
AUGUSTINE, SERMON 187, SECTION I, PART I

So, when Midnight Mass is ended, the turkey is cooked and the presents opened, let us give just a little time to savouring this mystery and, indeed, tasting and seeing how sweet God is.

Guidelines

This week leading up to Christmas is usually one of intense busyness, with (at least in my case) Christmas cards still to write, shopping still to do and carol service sheets still to put through the photocopier (which will, of course, jam at the most crucial or awkward moment). Amid this devout insanity, the scriptures this week have called us back to the priority—the Advent (from the Latin *ad ventus*, literally the 'coming towards us') of God. Again and again in the biblical passages that the Church sets before us in these final days, we are reminded of the initiative of God. When we feel under pressure from the need to meet a postal deadline or avoid a queue, when we see the vast array of tasks before us, it is easy to think that it's all our work and our doing: Christmas won't be OK unless I do everything right. Yet Advent and Christmas remind us that, in the words of Psalm 100:3, 'it is God who made us and not we ourselves'; we are not responsible for absolutely everything. It was God who, through the centuries, prepared his people to be able to receive his ultimate gift of himself in Jesus Christ; it was God who took the initiative in sending an angel to Mary; it was God who stopped Joseph giving up his new wife, God who directed the holy family into Egypt to escape the wrath of Herod.

If, having survived Christmas Day and reading this on the Sunday, it all seems a bit much and we can't think of anything to say in our prayers, then there's no need to say anything. Let's just sit or kneel and say simply 'Maranatha', 'Come, Lord', and allow God to take the initiative. It can seem at the time as if we are searching for God, as if we are working hard, holding on to God by our fingertips. If, when we die, we are given the grace of looking back over our lives, we shall see the reverse: our desire to hold on to God and our inspiration to work hard in our lives of faith were, in fact, gifts from God himself. He is the author of all holy desires, all good counsels and all just works. We feel it is our work because God wants us to feel involved and wants to share his life with us; yet when we pray, it is his Spirit praying in us (Romans 8:26), and a little silence helps us to know it.

1 The cost of God

Acts 7:54–60

In the secular calendar, Christmas has now ended and the great festival of The Sales has begun, when DFS adverts are interspersed with repeats of *The Sound of Music*. Having spent a fortune on Christmas, we are now invited to spend a further fortune in the sales. Saving all this money can be a costly business.

What the shops call Boxing Day, Christians have traditionally called St Stephen's Day (celebrated yesterday in the Church calendar). Stephen was the first martyr of Christianity and, at a time when we not unreasonably think about the beauty, comfort and consolation that our faith brings, the stoning of Stephen reminds us of the cost—not of the sales, but of God, the expense of discipleship. So often, contemporary atheist critics suggest that faith is a comfort blanket to shield us from the chilliness of the universe, or a crutch to make life more bearable for the weak and feeble. Nestled next to Christmas Day, the witness of Stephen to the point of death is a counterblast to that kind of easy, cheap assault.

Just before the section of Acts 7 that we are reading today, Stephen has outlined to the high priest and council their common history, illustrating how, again and again, their people have rejected the messengers and prophets of God. He places Jesus within that story as the last and greatest of the people rejected by those in authority. Not only does Stephen remind his contemporaries of their own history, but he makes sure they cannot pretend that there are other perfectly reasonable ways of reading that history. In our own day, too, many people read Western history as a story of grow-

134

ing liberation from the irrational tyranny of religion and monarchy towards the sunlit uplands of democracy, science and sweet reason. Leaving aside the fact that it's not true (the 20th century was both the most irreligious and the most violent in history), it is also far from being the only construal of the facts. Stephen's account of their common past infuriates the arbiters of truth on the council and they stone him to death. No one is yet stoning us to death for our account of the way things are, but to hear some modern critics of Christianity is definitely to hear the enraged grinding of teeth.

2 The children of God

Matthew 2:13–18

'Christmas is a time for the children' is a popular mantra. While, at one level, there is much to delight a child about the season, there is something in our repetition of this slogan that smacks of our disowning the festival for ourselves. The innocence and simplicity of the shepherds and the beasts in the stable, and the beautiful holiness of Jesus, Mary and Joseph, all suggest that this is a slightly make-believe occasion—lovely for the kids, but with nothing to say to the adults. Yet today, the third day after Christmas, is traditionally when Christians recall the the slaughter by King Herod's soldiers of all children under the age of two in Bethlehem. It is a stark reminder, amid the tinsel, of the threat that the newborn Jesus poses to those in power, and of the lengths to which any of us might go to defend our position. We may not have the manpower physically to slaughter people who threaten our way of life, but office politics and domestic disputes between neighbours turn outwardly mild people into underhand thugs. The decisions made even by democratically elected governments, in terms of who gets humanitarian assistance, what strings are attached to aid money and which despotic regimes we'll maintain and which we'll invade, have much to do with preserving our hegemony, usually at someone else's expense.

Some have suggested that Matthew invented the occasion of the slaughter so that he could demonstrate how Jesus fulfils Old Testament prophecies—Hosea's 'out of Egypt I have called my son' (11:1) and Jeremiah's prophecy of Rachel weeping in Ramah (31:15). Yet enough is known about Herod and about pagan ethics for his murdering of children to be entirely believable. Moreover, it is equally possible that the flight and slaughter inspired Matthew and the first Christians to search their scriptures for texts by which they could understand these extraordinary events—rather than inventing events to fit Hebrew prophecy—not least because neither prophecy is a neat fit. The angel of the Lord calls God's son into Egypt, not out of it, and Jeremiah instructs Rachel to stop weeping in the next verses (31:16–17), because her children are coming back from exile. Either way, however, all of a sudden Christmas seems much more adult.

3 The silence of God

Luke 2:15–20

I remember, as a particularly angular theological student, refusing to sing 'Away in a manger' on the grounds that the line 'no crying he makes' reeked of heresy, his supposed lack of tears suggesting that Jesus was less than fully human. I was very fierce in my desire to hunt down all docetism (the heresy that Jesus was essentially God dressed up as a man, not really a human being)! I've calmed down a little since then and now happily sing the carol at the family nativity service, assuming that the line in question just means he wasn't crying at that particular moment, probably because he was asleep.

What I've found much more striking in recent years (although it should have been obvious) is that, of course, Jesus says nothing in these early chapters. If he is both perfectly human and perfectly divine, two natures united as one person, then not only do we see a baby asleep in the feeding trough but we also see God. The shepherds make haste, presumably asking in every Bethlehem inn if there is a pregnant woman staying in the shed, and find the baby. They do not, however, find Jesus performing a miracle (unless his not crying is to be ascribed, pace John 2:11, as his first sign) or teaching a parable—yet they return praising and glorifying God. Presumably this is because what the angels had said turned out to be true, and because every newborn baby is a miracle and something for which to praise God.

For us, however, that praise and glory must also derive from the extraordinary sight of God silently asleep in the manger. Jesus promises always to be with his disciples (Matthew 28:20) and asks us to abide with and in him (John 15:9). Jesus' life being not only finite but also eternal, therefore,

Christmas is the time when we are reminded that he always abides with us, in part, as a baby—silently keeping us company, giving us a focus for our warmth and affection, not questioning or judging us but simply being lovingly with us. As he abides in Mary's bosom, he bids us abide with him in the bosom of his Father (John 1:18: the word 'heart' translates literally from the Greek as 'bosom'). This is our true home, the stable where our true life is born and we are warmly held.

4 The poor food of God

Luke 2:1–7

Just as Jesus promises to abide with us always, from birth to death, so he promises always to be our food. Supremely, he feeds us in the Eucharist, the source and summit of Christian worship, but he is always there as food in prayer, silence and scripture. This is clear from the earliest moments of Jesus' birth. He is born in Bethlehem, a word literally meaning 'house of bread', and he is laid by Mary in a manger, a feeding trough. This is a beautiful reflection for us at Christmas, as we discover that the bread of heaven (John 6:33), in whom we will be built up into a living building (1 Peter 2:5), is born in the 'house of bread'. He is placed in a feeding trough, reminding us not only of God's breathtaking humility but also that he comes to be ceaselessly available to everyone, food for the journey, enduring to eternal life. The manger from which the animals have fed now holds the one on whom we all will feed.

Jesus' simple availability in the manger opens our eyes additionally to his vulnerability and poverty. In these two days of calm before the new year, it is worth spending time reflecting on the nature of the Christian God. Bethlehem, as the prophet Micah (5:2) informs us, is the least of the clans of Judah; what will make her cease to be least is precisely the birth within her walls of the Messiah. The birth does not take place at home, or even in an inn, but among the animals—possibly even among ritually unclean animals such as mice and pigs, those that do not both chew the cud and have cloven hooves (Leviticus 11; Deuteronomy 14). Even more, of course, the reason for the family to be in Bethlehem is that they are being counted by an occupying army.

Yet in that manger has been born a new focus, a new release of God's energy and life in the world. The birth of Jesus in such circumstances tells us that even amid the most oppressed of circumstances and difficult of environments, God is free. He is quite capable of doing something new and he can give us an inner freedom also, regardless of external constraints, the kind exemplified by those could still sing the psalms in the camps at Auschwitz and Dachau.

5 The love of God

John 15:12–17

How are we to respond to the angry, the violent, the oppressive powers of this world? The apostle and Gospel writer John gives us the theological base for the way Stephen responded (see Day 1 above): he forgave his accusers and loved them. Of all the New Testament writers, John is surely best characterised as the apostle of love. Both in his Gospel and in his letters, he returns frequently to love as the basis for Christian living. 'Love' is one of those words, like 'hope' and 'faith', that have been ruined by the modern world. To many ears, hope is equivalent to optimism, and faith to blind belief in the improbable. Love, equally, means either sex or letting people do whatever they want—society echoing the teenage argument that 'if you loved me, you'd let me do x, y or z'.

Augustine, in his seventh sermon on the letters of John, says, 'Love, and do what you will'. This is not patristic cover for indulgence; it means simply, as Augustine goes on to say in that sermon, 'let the root of love be within, of this root can nothing spring but what is good'. If we truly love, he says, then our wills are always right and we shall only do what is good. Stephen loved his accusers, which did not mean letting them think whatever they fancied (he argues very strongly to them) or pretending that what they were doing was not wrong. It did mean, however, asking God not to hold their sin against them, and not responding with violence himself.

One of the reasons so many people are afraid of religion is that they fear that disagreeing with someone must be a violent act. Christians will frequently hold strong opinions, which will appear all the stronger to others as the framework of society ceases to be Judeo-Christian. What should be so distinctive about us, however, is our holding them with love, not ceasing to bless those who curse us, and providing care, education and charity to all, regardless of their beliefs. We do not respond to society with either 'Jesus is Lord, and I'll use every means at my disposal to force you to agree' or 'Jesus is Lord, but that's just my personal opinion'; we respond with 'Jesus is Lord, which is why I love you'.

6 The youth of God

Revelation 21:6

Whether it is the iconic painting of God the Father touching Adam in the Sistine Chapel or the picture in our imaginations, God is almost always portrayed as old. Almightiness, Kingliness, Fatherliness, Lordliness: so many of our attributes of God seem instinctively old, not least because we think that our understanding of what it means to be a father, for example, should then be mapped on to God rather than the other way round. As Paul tells the people of Ephesus, however, 'every fatherhood in heaven and on earth takes its name' from the Fatherhood of God (3:14–15), not the reverse. It is important to know this when, say, our own experience of being fathered means that we find it difficult to relate warmly to God as Father. We need to stop writing pale, fallen human fatherhood on to God and allow his perfect Fatherhood, as the father some may never have had, to be written on to human parenting.

The Christmas scene, however, tells us something immensely important for our image of God—that God is not old, but rather young. The old man in a beard is suddenly replaced in our minds by the young baby in a manger. One reason why people paint Christianity as irrelevant is that they think God is incredibly old, because he's been around for ever. God, though, is eternal, and eternity is not just lots and lots of time but, rather, something beyond time. God has been around for ever, yet he has also only just arrived; being eternal means that age and time do not affect him, so he is eternally young. As Jesus says three times in the Revelation to John, he is both the beginning and the end, the alpha and the omega (1:8; 21:6; 22:13); he is not just the oldest but is also the newest.

On this New Year's Day, we may catalogue our many failed resolutions and feel that we are getting older and getting nowhere. The babe in the manger and the alpha and omega of Revelation recall us to a different truth—that the eternally youthful God is as thrilled and excited by us now as he was when we were not even born. Even more, because God is not only the love from whom we come but also the love to whom we are going, this year we are journeying towards our youth, and towards a share in eternity. So we can grasp hold of 2011 with confidence and hope.

Guidelines

The first week of this fortnight of reflections considered God's desire for us and his taking the initiative in pursuing us. We saw also, through the words and actions of Mary, John, Zechariah and Isaiah, how he stirs up our desire for him, and that all we need do in response to his longing is to wait and say 'yes'. Our waiting was vindicated on Christmas Day in the most amazing way imaginable, and this last week has been lived in the light of that vindication—exploring the love, silence, nourishment and youthfulness of the incarnation, but also the cost, the maturity and the poverty it compels. For the secular world, Christmas began in September and ended on Boxing Day; for Christians, it began on Christmas Day and lasts not just for twelve days until Epiphany, but for 40 days until Jesus is presented in the temple by his parents (Luke 2:22–35).

It is easy to rush into the new year, shoving the baubles into a cupboard and moving straight on to the January sales, booking the summer holiday and preparing for the next school term. The miracle of the incarnation, however, cannot even begin to be comprehended in a few days, pondered while the leftover turkey is turned into curry and salad. God spent many centuries preparing his people to receive this gift, giving them enough words, and expanding their hearts and minds so that they would be capable of receiving Jesus. So let us, as this new year unfolds, allow ourselves time to luxuriate in and explore the miracle of the Word made flesh, that its great light may illuminate the whole year.

FURTHER READING

M. Boulding, *The Coming of God* (SCM Canterbury Press, 2001)
H. McCabe, *The Good Life: Ethics and the Pursuit of Happiness* (Continuum, 2005).

The BRF

Magazine

Richard Fisher writes...

'Give up the ghost', 'out of the mouths of babes and sucklings', 'the writing's on the wall', 'the powers that be', 'the spirit is will-ing, but the flesh is weak', 'the blind leading the blind'... all of these phrases are in com-mon usage today, but did you know that they come straight from the King James Version of the Bible, first published in 1611? Next year marks its 400th anniversary and exciting plans have been developing over the past two years to make 2011 a year of celebration of the Bible in the English language. The celebrations have two core strands.

The 2011 Trust (www.2011trust.org) is focusing on the arts, heritage and education, and as a result a wide range of initiatives will be taking place throughout the year—including conferences, lectures, exhibitions and celebrations of the Bible in art, music and film. BRF's particular involvement will be with primary schools, providing a new In-Service Training session for teachers on using the Bible with children in the classroom, and a new version of our creative arts-based Barnabas RE Day theme, 'What's so special about the Bible?'

The second strand is 'Biblefresh' (www.biblefresh.com), a multi-organisation collaboration led by the Evangelical Alliance, intended to stimulate and resource churches to engage afresh with the Bible and its message. You can read more about it on the following pages.

We'd like to hear your stories and reflections. What does the Bible mean to you? How has it influenced your life? Is there a particular Bible verse or passage that is significant to you? Would you be willing to share this with us? Are there particular books or resources that have helped you in your reading and exploration of the Bible, which you'd like to commend to others? During 2011 we'd like to collect these stories and comments and publish them on our website. Your own experiences and insights could be a great help and inspiration to others.

We're excited by the way so many organisations and individuals are supporting the plans for 2011, and we encourage you and your church to get involved too. Who knows what an impact this might have?

Richard Fisher, Chief Executive

Biblefresh

Rob Cotton

biblefresh
It could change your world

Knowledge of the Bible seems to be vanishing fast in the UK, according to a recent Durham University survey. A bemused 60 per cent of the general public couldn't recall anything about the parable of the good Samaritan, and a third of under-45s (for whom Bible awareness seemed weakest) scratched their heads to remember anything about the feeding of the five thousand.

Against this background, perhaps it's unsurprising that Christians, too, face increasing difficulties in engaging with the Bible—but an exciting new campaign is aiming to reverse the trend.

The campaign 'Biblefresh' will encourage people to take another look at the Bible, to engage with scripture in ways that will transform their relationship with the Bible, enabling real experiences of spiritual renewal.

As Bible Society's Senior Campaign Manager, I have been seconded to Evangelical Alliance as the Network Coordinator for Biblefresh, to envision churches and organisations. I am genuinely excited about Biblefresh and the opportunity to mobilise churches in discovering fresh approaches that bring release from any sense of guilt or failure, and aid new understanding. God still speaks through his word today.

Biblefresh begins in churches preparing themselves in prayer during Advent this year and will climax in a year-long campaign in 2011—all with the aim of giving Christians a new confidence and excitement about using scripture. 2011 is the 400th anniversary of the King James Version of the Bible. This has provided a focus for the campaign, which is currently gathering real momentum, with the Methodist Church nationally designating 2011 'Biblefresh—The year of the Bible' and other denominations and networks doing the same.

It is important that churches launch Biblefresh effectively in the new year, inviting church members to covenant to engage with the Bible in new ways during the year. There will be high points of the campaign around the Christian festivals, focusing upon 'the Cross' at Easter, 'Communication' to people in their own heart language at Pentecost and 'Carnivals' over the summer, 'Cultivation' of God's word throughout the season of harvest, and finally 'Christmas' as the climax of the year.

Some 50 Christian agencies and colleges are already behind the Evangelical Alliance-led initiative, with BRF, Bible Society, Scripture Union and Wycliffe Bible translators among the key partners. But it is important that those who love scripture and engage with its life-changing message make the most of the opportunities during the Biblefresh campaign to share the word of God with others and invite them to share in the Bible experiences.

The campaign will offer churches four streams of involvement. These are Bible reading (new publications are being developed and public reading events are being organised), Bible training (with major festivals already preparing to offer a programme in keeping with the campaign, courses and Bible boot camps), Bible translation (into our 21st-century culture as well as languages around the world) and Bible experience (using film, music, drama, fine arts and exhibitions). The specially designed website www.biblefresh.com will keep churches updated with the latest campaign news and resources, and a further website, www.2011trust.org, gives information on civic events and arts initiatives.

> *… to share the word of God with others…*

There have already been some significant events to prepare the church for Biblefresh, in two envisioning tours with musicians Paul Field and Dan Wheeler, plus Australian band Sons of Korah, who have creatively set the Psalms to music. The Sons of Korah's impact, singing scripture to an audience, has been amazing to see, and no doubt their tour will be a highlight of the Biblefresh campaign.

Biblefresh will enable organisations to profile their resources, and readers can look forward to new and exciting initiatives that will encourage, challenge and renew their passion for the word of God.

Envisioning events have given church leaders the full picture to pass on to their congregations, and the events have featured well-known Bible champions who are supporting the campaign. There is also a resources handbook for churches, to envision leaders and church members to make the most of Biblefresh. This handbook is a must-read publication.

'Biblefresh: It could change your world'—your personal world or the wider world, as people apply the message to their lives.

For further information, contact Revd Rob Cotton (rob.cotton@biblesociety.org.uk; Tel: 07766 075486) or Alexandra Lilley (a.lilley@eauk.org; Tel: 020 7207 2109)

The Revd Rob Cotton is Senior Campaign Manager at Bible Society

An interview with Heather Fenton

Heather Fenton is a priest in the Church in Wales and has run the retreat house, Coleg y Groes , for 25 years. In September 2009 she became editor of *Quiet Spaces*, BRF's prayer and spirituality journal. Rachel Walker, BRF's Marketing Coordinator, spoke to Heather and asked her about her life and how she came to be editing *Quiet Spaces*.

How did you get to where you are today?

I became a Christian when I was 15, although, like many children in the early 1960s, I had some residual Christian faith before that, and had been confirmed because there were classes at the independent school at which I was a 'day girl'. I was in the Youth Fellowship at the local village church in west Kent, and when I became a Christian I joined the choir as an excuse for going to church. About 18 months later, I had an experience of the baptism of the Holy Spirit, which was very controversial at the time, and over which I had quite a hard time.

Early on, I realised that God had a special calling for each one of us, and I looked round to see what that might be for me. As I was good at art, I decided that perhaps I should go to art school. So this is what I did when I left school, and that's how I got into my career in publishing.

While at art school, I specialised in lettering (hand-drawn lettering is my speciality, although I don't do much at the moment) and typography. Afterwards I worked for publishers, including Routledge and OUP, initially producing their publicity material but going on to work in their Production Departments. As I wanted to have a better theological understanding, I began to think and pray about going to theological college. In 1976 I was made redundant and took the opportunity to go to Trinity College in Bristol to study theology. I then went back into publishing for another eight years, and ended up as a Production Manager. It was then that God moved me to rural Wales and, together with some friends, I set up the retreat house Coleg y Groes. This is now in its 25th year and has been used by God for a great many people during that time.

Where is your ministry based?

I was ordained in the Church in Wales as a deacon in 1987 and as a priest ten years later. I have served in a number of parishes in this remote rural deanery over the last 23 years. At the time of writing, I am vicar of two rural parishes, small in number and massive in terms of area. They are Welsh-speaking sheep-farming areas. I am well known for my innovative worship services and my work with primary school-age children, and am a school chaplain as well as a governor.

What is your current role in publishing?

I have helped the Church in Wales with the production of some of their publications. I am currently Editor of the Church of England magazine for Lay Readers (licensed lay ministers) called *The Reader* and have been appointed as the new editor of *Quiet Spaces*. This latter role brings together my experience in running a retreat house with my long career in publishing. I always think God is good at making the best use of resources!

> *God is good at making the best use of resources*

What have been the main influences on your own spiritual journey?

The evangelical wing of the Anglican church, plus the charismatic movement (Fountain Trust, for example), as well as the Fisherfolk and the associated community movement, which started at the Church of the Holy Redeemer in Houston, Texas, and spread to the UK (Cumbrae in Scotland and Post Green in Dorset) in the 1960s and '70s, were all very influential for me. Now I am a founder member of quite a small dispersed community, 'The Community of Coleg y Groes', associated with the retreat house ministry I have had for the last 24 years. Ten years ago I took an MA in Celtic Christianity, which was very stimulating and a great blessing.

What are you hoping to do in the future?

I am planning to retire from parish work and to sell Coleg y Groes, but to stay in Wales. I will be working for the Church of England and BRF, and may well produce some publications of my own. I also want to do some more art, especially using texture and lettering images, and I have a vegetable patch.

Heather Fenton is editor of Quiet Spaces *and a priest in the Church in Wales. This year's issues of* Quiet Spaces *are entitled 'Yesterday', 'Today' and 'Tomorrow'.*

The People's Bible

Martyn Payne

As you will have read elsewhere in this issue, Christians are gearing up for a big celebration next year. 2011 marks the 400th anniversary of the publication of the Authorised (King James) Bible—the Bible in the language of the people—which has had such a radical impact on the life and culture of our nation and, through the work of missionaries and the expansion of the British Empire, on the whole world. The Barnabas Children's Ministry team is not going to miss out on this moment! Plans are well under way to use the anniversary as a springboard for our work in primary schools across the UK in 2011.

In the course of the last decade, Barnabas in Schools has become a respected and valued partner in support of the teaching of Religious Education in our primary schools. Well over 800 of our unique RE Days have been enjoyed by thousands of children as we have endeavoured to explore Christianity creatively and opened up the Bible with mime, drama, music, dance and various storytelling styles. Building on this platform, BRF and the Barnabas children's team have been working with the 2011 Trust and will be taking a lead in the delivery of some specially designed RE Days; these days will help children to unpack both the spiritual and the cultural legacy of the King James Bible. We have also been given funding to offer INSET sessions for teachers to Anglican dioceses in the country, which will explore the story of the Bible and look at creative ways to share it with children. This God-given opportunity is a very exciting project indeed, and one that the Barnabas children's team, with its experience and proven track record, is well placed to deliver.

> *Over 800 of our unique RE Days have been enjoyed by thousands of children*

To pick up a copy of the Authorised Version of the Bible and open its double-columned pages may not seem like anything special to us today, but 400 years ago, in 1611, doing just this was nothing short of a revolution. It opened up a whole new world of possibilities and led to changes in thinking that shaped the course of history and the culture of the Western world. This one book has left a lasting legacy, right up to the present day.

Just imagine. Being able to read the Bible in your own language, English, in 1611 was like… the first time our generation logged on to the Internet: suddenly a whole new world of information and ideas was at its fingertips. It was like… the first time our generation used an iPhone to speak to and even see friends and relatives overseas: suddenly a whole new world of communications and contacts was available. It was like… the first time our generation, while watching live TV, was able to influence the outcome of events by pressing a red button: suddenly a whole new world of influence and power could be accessed by ordinary men and women, who until then had received everything second-hand and at a disabling distance. So you can see why this anniversary is well worth celebrating!

> *God's words in the Authorised Version leapt off the page and had a profound impact*

Alongside the special RE Days and INSET sessions, a resource booklet called *The People's Bible* will be published by Barnabas, including the background story to the publication of the King James Bible and its influence, as well as suggestions for classroom activities. There are also plans to produce a DVD of members of our team demonstrating some of the lesson ideas.

There is always, of course, the danger that an anniversary like this might end up just looking backwards. But although it is right and proper to mark this significant historical moment, when that moment has to do with the living word of God, there is no way it can remain as history. God's words in the Authorised Version leapt off the page and had a profound impact on the lives and culture of the people of that day. As Christians, we believe that this still can be true today. The challenge for the Barnabas ministry team is to present children with Bible stories that are not just for then but for *them*!

The 'for ever' but also 'for now' dimension of the words of scripture is very familiar to the Barnabas children's ministry team is very familiar. Our aim has always been to take the 'timeless' truths of the Bible and find creative ways to make them 'timely' for the children. Children do not suffer religious language or disconnected learning gladly, so we have always needed to make the Bible relevant to our own time and culture, just as the brave translators 400 years ago did when they approached the Greek and Latin manuscripts before them. What miracles happened then, and still do happen, when we let scripture breathe like this! As a team, we have lost count of the number of times children's responses on our RE Days have taken us by surprise, revealing new insights into the stories as well as reminding us of a child's God-given gift to the church—namely, to teach us how to enter the kingdom of God. All of you who have ever worked with children have, I am sure, had the same experiences.

> *A child's God-given gift to the church—to teach us how to enter the kingdom of God*

Celebrating the impact of *The People's Bible* with primary school children and their teachers next year will be a privilege. Do pray for us as we introduce them to the Bible—a Book of Books that is not only a window into God's work with people in the past, but also a mirror in which we can discover God at work with us today.

For more information about *The People's Bible* and the special RE Days for children and INSET for teachers in 2011, please contact Lynda Ward, the Barnabas Team Administrator: barnabas@brf.org.uk; tel: 01865 319704.

Martyn Payne is a member of the Barnabas children's ministry team, based in London.

Recommended reading

Naomi Starkey

Time and again, we hear media reports about today's anonymous society, in which no one looks out for their neighbour or feels any sense of responsibility for what goes on beyond their front door. For better or worse, a church or chapel building is a highly visible symbol of people coming together for a common purpose.

People come along to their local church for a variety of reasons. Of course, it is often because they are already Christians and want a place where they can worship—or they may be seeking God and (rightly) reckon that attending a church service is a good starting point. More than a few, however, come in search of a sense of belonging, some kind of community, and this search may not necessarily be linked to an active faith. As a result, it creates tremendous opportunities for witness and ministry but also great responsibilities in terms of pastoral care.

In *Growing a Caring Church*, Wendy Billington draws on her years of pastoral work in the community and in the local church, to share ways in which Christians can not only care for one another but also extend this care to people in the wider neighbourhood. Her role as coordinator of the pastoral care programme in a large church includes providing training in pastoral skills, listening to people's concerns, bereavement care, marriage enrichment and supporting cancer sufferers and their families.

When leadership resources are already stretched, pastoral care is an area in which it is all too easy to fall short, with potentially disastrous consequences. And if a church cannot nurture its own members, how can it hope to be strong enough to care for anyone else? Aware of this challenge, Wendy shows how church home groups can be places where people's pain and difficulties are noticed, and first steps are taken to help. Following Jesus' command that as his disciples we are to love one another and also share his love with the world, we can learn how to offer the kind of wise and practical assistance that will start to guide those who are struggling back towards wholeness of life.

A crucial skill in all kinds of pastoral care is the art of listening, something that is in danger of being lost in our noisy, stressed and superficial world. We forget about listening not only to others but also to God, to ourselves, to our communities—and even to the needs of our planet. If we do not listen, we cannot hope to grow in wisdom, to deepen relationships with others or to share our faith in sensitive and appropriate ways.

BRF are pleased to be publishing a new edition of Michael Mitton's *A Heart to Listen*, which explores how, with God's help, we can relearn this essential art. Michael interweaves biblical reflection with insights from many years of listening ministry in the UK and abroad. To speak to heart as well as head, he concludes each chapter with an episode from a creative story that tells of people listening and learning from one another in a challenging crosscultural setting.

Now a freelance writer and consultant, Michael headed up the Christian Listeners ministry of the Acorn Christian Healing Foundation (where he was also deputy director) for a number of years, before working as Diocesan Mission and Ministry Development Adviser for Derby diocese. He has also written *A Handful of Light* and *Restoring the Woven Cord* (new edition) for BRF, and is a contributor to *New Daylight* Bible reading notes.

He wrote *A Heart to Listen* not only because of his belief in the importance of this skill for every area of Christian discipleship but also to encourage people to take first steps in developing it for themselves. In his preface for the new edition, he shares something of the reaction he has received to the book, including an email about its effect on one reader: 'She wrote, "I want to say thank you for your wonderful but disturbing book. It made me weep and laugh out loud; it gave me such hope and joy. A lot of changes are happening at our local church and not without much heartache and soul-searching. Your book has given me confidence to see things through with the grace of our Lord and the love and compassion that he has given me for people."'

Learning to listen draws us into the heart of God

He continues: 'On the days when I struggle with confidence and wish I was a better writer, I go back to emails like this and realise that something of my message has actually got through in this book. The message is essentially very simple: learning to listen draws us into the heart of God, to feel something of the compassion and care that he feels for the humans he has created. When we encounter this, it affects everything.'

To order a copy of any of these books, please turn to page 159.

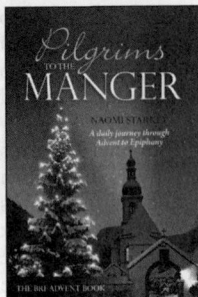

An extract from
Pilgrims to the Manger

BRF's Advent book for 2010, written by *New Daylight* editor Naomi Starkey, is an invitation to a pilgrimage through Advent, Christmas and Epiphany. In the following extract, the Introduction to the book, Naomi explains the imagery on which the book is based and offers us both refreshment and challenge as we take up the invitation to journey with her.

'Christmas isn't what it used to be!' I was twelve years old, sitting on my bed, tears trickling down my cheeks as I gazed out in a melodramatic verge-of-adolescence way at the rooftops of suburban Cambridge. My mother hovered in the doorway, trying to make sense of my mood amid the 1001 tasks of a family Christmas Eve.

While I had known for years that there was no Father Christmas (although I pretended, to keep my younger siblings happy), what triggered my despair was finding that I no longer felt the magic. *I wasn't excited any more.* I knew the stories of baby Jesus inside out and back to front; I was still up and about when my mother was filling the stockings; I knew that Christmas dinner was followed by mountains of washing up. I would go to bed on 24 December, wake up next morning and, yes, there would be presents—but in the end it was just another day, followed by the next, and the next.

Thankfully, life has moved on in all kinds of ways since then. I have come to realise the difference between knowing Bible stories and understanding their message; I have learned the pleasures of giving as well as receiving; I have discovered the blessed invention that is the dishwasher. When my own daughter was born at the end of November one year, she appeared as the Christmas morning sermon illustration—and I found that all the carols about mother and baby acquired special resonance.

Christmases continue to come and go, though, and each year the turn of the seasons seems to happen faster. The round-robin letters, which I for one always enjoy, start to change. Instead of announcing the latest baby, music exam grade or Brownie badge, the news is of children starting to scatter from the family home to further education, jobs or travel. For my parents' generation, there is the shock of familiar names beginning to disappear from the Christmas card list, couples of names dwindling to one on its own. The letters are increasingly dominated by health issues and the upheavals of retirement and downsizing.

It may be, too, that as we try to sum up our news for family and friends, we face the uncomfortable truth that life hasn't turned out quite as we expected. Somehow or other, we never did get that promotion. Yes, our marriage held together but we keep thinking about that old flame we met at the school reunion. Thanks to the economic climate, our dreams of trading up to a more commodious house have evaporated, at least for now. Then there's our relationship with God. Yes, we go to a lovely church but somehow the worship doesn't touch us in the same way any more. Same old hymns, same old Bible readings, same old sermons that leave us feeling vaguely—or sometimes specifically—guilty. And, dare we say it to ourselves, 'Same old God'?

This book of readings is an invitation to pilgrimage, to accompany me through the weeks of Advent, to Christmas itself and on to Epiphany. As the days and weeks pass, we will reflect together on a range of issues—the significance of the festivities, the deeper values that underpin our lives, some of the other special days in the Church calendar at this season, and how we can begin to deepen our understanding of God's perspective on our world, our church and ourselves.

> *A pilgrimage of both head and heart*

'Pilgrimage' is more than a figure of speech in this book, however. I invite you to join an imaginary group of pilgrims whose path takes them from a city centre high street, out to the suburbs, beyond the city to a mountain top (don't worry—it's not very high), and then back into the city to find the cathedral, where we rest for the celebrations surrounding Christmas Day itself. In the following days, we travel beyond the streets and down to the sea, where this book concludes. It's not a conventional pilgrimage. It does not follow a well-trodden route to a well-known destination, although we will pass familiar landmarks; it is a pilgrimage of both head and heart in that our aim is to learn more of God and allow ourselves to be challenged by what we discover as we journey together. Above all, we will discover the truth of Immanuel: God is here, everywhere, present with us, if only we will look up and notice him walking alongside us.

Naomi Starkey is Commissioning Editor for BRF's adult list and edits and writes for New Daylight. *She has also written* Good Enough Mother *for BRF. To order either of her books, please turn to the order form on page 159.*

Guidelines © BRF 2010

The Bible Reading Fellowship
15 The Chambers, Vineyard, Abingdon OX14 3FE
Tel: 01865 319700; Fax: 01865 319701
E-mail: enquiries@brf.org.uk; Website: www.brf.org.uk

ISBN 978 1 84101 558 3

Distributed in Australia by Willow Connection, PO Box 288, Brookvale, NSW 2100.
Tel: 02 9948 3957; Fax: 02 9948 8153;
E-mail: info@willowconnection.com.au
Available also from all good Christian bookshops in Australia.
For individual and group subscriptions in Australia:
Mrs Rosemary Morrall, PO Box W35, Wanniassa, ACT 2903.

Distributed in New Zealand by Scripture Union Wholesale, PO Box 760, Wellington
Tel: 04 385 0421; Fax: 04 384 3990; E-mail: suwholesale@clear.net.nz

Publications distributed to more than 60 countries

Acknowledgments

The New Revised Standard Version of the Bible, Anglicized Edition, copyright © 1989, 1995 by the
Division of Christian Education of the National Council of the Churches of Christ in the USA.
Used by permission. All rights reserved.

The Holy Bible, New International Version, copyright © 1973, 1978, 1984, 1995 by International
Bible Society. Used by permission of Hodder & Stoughton Publishers, a member of the
Hachette Livre UK Group. All rights reserved. 'NIV' is a registered trademark of International
Bible Society. UK trademark number 1448790.

The New Jerusalem Bible, published and copyright © 1985 by Darton, Longman and Todd Ltd
and les Editions du Cerf, and by Doubleday, a division of Bantam Doubleday Dell Publishing
Group, Inc. Used by permission of Darton, Longman and Todd Ltd, and Doubleday, a division
of Random house, Inc.

Revised Grail Psalms copyright © 2008, Conception Abbey/The Grail, admin. by GIA
Publications, Inc., www.giamusic.com. All rights reserved.

Printed in Singapore by Craft Print International Ltd

SUPPORTING BRF'S MINISTRY

As a Christian charity, BRF is involved in five distinct yet complementary areas.

- **BRF** (www.brf.org.uk) resources adults for their spiritual journey through Bible reading notes, books, and a programme of quiet days and teaching days. BRF also provides the infrastructure that supports our other four specialist ministries.
- **Foundations21** (www.foundations21.org.uk) provides flexible and innovative ways for individuals and groups to explore their Christian faith and discipleship through a multimedia internet-based resource.
- **Messy Church**, led by Lucy Moore (www.messychurch.org.uk), enables churches all over the UK (and increasingly abroad) to reach children and adults beyond the fringes of the church .
- **Barnabas in Churches** (www.barnabasinchurches.org.uk) helps churches to support, resource and develop their children's ministry with the under-11s more effectively .
- **Barnabas in Schools** (www.barnabasinschools.org.uk) enables primary school children and teachers to explore Christianity creatively and bring the Bible alive within RE and Collective Worship.

At the heart of BRF's ministry is a desire to equip adults and children for Christian living—helping them to read and understand the Bible, to explore prayer and to grow as disciples of Jesus. We need your help to make a real impact on the local church, local schools and the wider community.

- You could support BRF's ministry with a donation or standing order (using the response form overleaf).
- You could consider making a bequest to BRF in your will.
- You could encourage your church to support BRF as part of your church's giving to home mission—perhaps focusing on a specific area of our ministry, or a particular member of our Barnabas team.
- Most important of all, you could support BRF with your prayers.

If you would like to discuss how a specific gift or bequest could be used in the development of our ministry, please phone 01865 319700 or email enquiries@brf.org.uk.

Whatever you can do or give, we thank you for your support.

BRF MINISTRY APPEAL RESPONSE FORM

Name _____

Address _____

_____ Postcode _____

Telephone _____ Email _____
(tick as appropriate)

Gift Aid Declaration

❏ I am a UK taxpayer. I want BRF to treat as Gift Aid Donations all donations I make from 6 April 2000 until I notify you otherwise.

Signature _____ Date _____

❏ I would like to support BRF's ministry with a regular donation by standing order (please complete the Banker's Order below).

Standing Order – Banker's Order

To the Manager, Name of Bank/Building Society

Address _____

_____ Postcode _____

Sort Code _____ Account Name _____

Account No _____

Please pay Royal Bank of Scotland plc, Drummonds, 49 Charing Cross, London SW1A 2DX (Sort Code 16-00-38), for the account of BRF A/C No. 00774151

The sum of _____ pounds on ___ /___ /___ (insert date your standing order starts) and thereafter the same amount on the same day of each month until further notice.

Signature _____ Date _____

Single donation

❏ I enclose my cheque/credit card/Switch card details for a donation of £5 £10 £25 £50 £100 £250 (other) £ _____ to support BRF's ministry

Credit/Switch card no. ⬚⬚⬚⬚ ⬚⬚⬚⬚ ⬚⬚⬚⬚ ⬚⬚⬚⬚ ⬚⬚⬚⬚

Expires ⬚⬚⬚⬚ Security code ⬚⬚⬚ Issue no. (Switch only) ⬚⬚⬚⬚

Signature _____ Date _____
(Where appropriate, on receipt of your donation, we will send you a Gift Aid form)

❏ Please send me information about making a bequest to BRF in my will.

Please detach and send this completed form to: Richard Fisher, BRF, 15 The Chambers, Vineyard, Abingdon OX14 3FE. BRF is a Registered Charity (No.233280)

GL 0310

BIBLE READING RESOURCES PACK

An updated pack of resources and ideas to help to promote Bible reading in your church is available from BRF. The pack, which will be of use at any time during the year (but especially for Bible Sunday in October), includes sample readings from BRF's Bible reading notes and *The People's Bible Commentary*, and lots of ideas for promoting Bible reading in your church.

Unless you specify the month in which you would like the pack sent, we will send it immediately on receipt of your order. The pack is free if despatched to a UK address (but if you would like to make a donation towards the cost, we will greatly appreciate it). If you require a pack sent outside the UK, please contact us and we will quote for postage and packing. We welcome your comments about the contents of the pack and your ideas for future ones.

This coupon should be sent to:

BRF
15 The Chambers
Vineyard
Abingdon
OX14 3FE

Name _____

Address _____

_____

_____ Postcode _____

Telephone _____

Email _____

Please send me _____ Bible Reading Resources Pack(s)

Please send the pack now/ in _____ (month).

I enclose a donation for £ _____ towards the cost of the pack.

BRF is a Registered Charity

❏ ...ease send me a Bible reading resources pack

❏ I would like to take out a subscription myself (complete your name and address details only once)

❏ I would like to give a gift subscription (please complete both name and address sections below)

Your name _____

Your address _____

_____ Postcode _____

Tel _____ Email _____

Gift subscription name _____

Gift subscription address _____

_____ Postcode _____

Gift message (20 words max.) _____

Please send *Guidelines* beginning with the January / May / September 2011
issue: (delete as applicable)

(please tick box)

	UK	SURFACE	AIR MAIL
GUIDELINES	❏ £14.40	❏ £15.90	❏ £19.20
GUIDELINES 3-year sub	❏ £36.00		
GUIDELINES pdf version	❏ £11.40 (UK and overseas)		
GUIDELINES printed + *New Daylight* by email	❏ £23.40	❏ £24.90	❏ £28.20

Confirm your email address _____

Please complete the payment details below and send, with appropriate
payment, to: **BRF, 15 The Chambers, Vineyard, Abingdon OX14 3FE.**

Total enclosed £ _____ (cheques should be made payable to 'BRF')

Please charge my Visa ❏ Mastercard ❏ Switch card ❏ with £ _____

Card number ❏❏❏❏❏❏❏❏❏❏❏❏❏❏❏❏❏❏❏❏

Expires ❏❏❏❏ Security code ❏❏❏ Issue no (Switch only) ❏❏❏❏

Signature (essential if paying by credit/Switch) _____

BRF is a Registered Charity

GL 0310

Please ensure that you complete and send off both sides of this order form.

Please send me the following book(s):

		Quantity	Price	Total
709 9	Pilgrims to the Manger (N. Starkey)		£7.99	
612 2	Good Enough Mother (N. Starkey)		£5.99	
799 0	Growing a Caring Church (W. Billington)		£6.99	
747 1	A Heart to Listen (M. Mitton)		£8.99	8.99
800 3	Restoring the Woven Cord (M. Mitton)		£8.99	
247 6	A Handful of Light (M. Mitton)		£7.99	
503 3	Messy Church (L. Moore)		£8.99	
725 9	Countdown to Christmas with Timothy Bear (B. Sears)		£6.99	
821 8	Ten Little Sheep (J. Godfrey)		£6.99	6.99
822 5	Joseph's Story of Christmas (G. Guadagno)		£5.99	5.99
659 7	Quiet Spaces: Yesterday (H. Fenton)		£4.99	
660 3	Quiet Spaces: Today (H. Fenton)		£4.99	
661 0	Quiet Spaces: Tomorrow (H. Fenton) (avail. November)		£4.99	
314 5	PBC: Genesis (G. West)		£8.99	
031 1	PBC: Psalms 1—72 (D. Coggan)		£8.99	
027 4	PBC: Luke (H. Wansbrough)		£7.99	
082 3	PBC: Romans (J.D.G. Dunn)		£8.99	

Total cost of books £ 21.97

Donation £

Postage and packing £ 2.25

TOTAL £ 24.22

POSTAGE AND PACKING CHARGES				
order value	UK	Europe	Surface	Air Mail
£7.00 & under	£1.25	£3.00	£3.50	£5.50
£7.01–£30.00	£2.25	£5.50	£6.50	£10.00
Over £30.00	free	prices on request		

For more information about new books and special offers, visit www.brfonline.org.uk. See over for payment details. All prices are correct at time of going to press, are subject to the prevailing rate of VAT and may be subject to change without prior warning.

PAYMENT DETAILS

Please complete the payment details below and send with appropriate payment and completed order form to:

BRF, 15 The Chambers, Vineyard, Abingdon OX14 3FE

Name _____

Address _____

_____ Postcode _____

Telephone _____

Email _____

Total enclosed £ _____ (cheques should be made payable to 'BRF')

Please charge my Visa ❑ Mastercard ❑ Switch card ❑ with £_____

Card number: ⬜⬜⬜⬜⬜⬜⬜⬜⬜⬜⬜⬜⬜⬜⬜⬜⬜⬜⬜

Expires ⬜⬜⬜⬜ Security code ⬜⬜⬜ Issue no (Switch only) ⬜⬜⬜⬜

Signature (essential if paying by credit/Switch) _____

❑ Please do not send me further information about BRF publications.

ALTERNATIVE WAYS TO ORDER

Christian bookshops: All good Christian bookshops stock BRF publications. For your nearest stockist, please contact BRF.

Telephone: The BRF office is open between 09.15 and 17.30. To place your order, phone 01865 319700; fax 01865 319701.

Web: Visit www.brf.org.uk

BRF is a Registered Charity

GL 0310